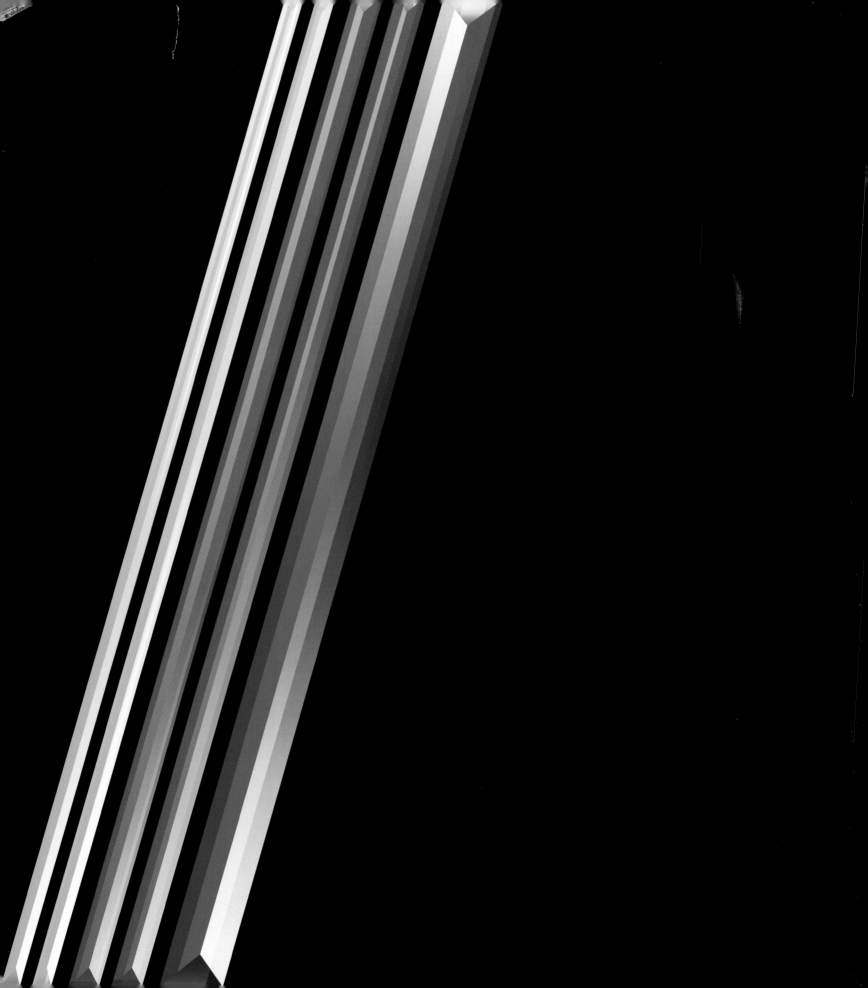

NASCAR 75TH
1948   2023
ANNIVERSARY

NASCAR
75 YEARS

KELLY CRANDALL / JIMMY CREED / MIKE HEMBREE / AL PEARCE

motorbooks

Inspiring | Educating | Creating | Entertaining

Brimming with creative inspiration, how-to projects, and useful information to enrich your everyday life, quarto.com is a favorite destination for those pursuing their interests and passions.

First Published in 2022 by Motorbooks, an imprint of The Quarto Group,
100 Cummings Center, Suite 265-D, Beverly, MA 01915, USA.
T (978) 282-9590 F (978) 283-2742 Quarto.com

Motorbooks titles are also available at discount for retail, wholesale, promotional, and bulk purchase. For details, contact the Special Sales Manager by email at specialsales@quarto.com or by mail at The Quarto Group, Attn: Special Sales Manager, 100 Cummings Center, Suite 265-D, Beverly, MA 01915, USA.

26 25 24 23 22   1 2 3 4 5

ISBN: 978-0-7603-8005-5

Digital edition published in 2022
eISBN: 978-0-7603-8006-2

Library of Congress Cataloging-in-Publication Data

Names: Crandall, Kelly, author. | Creed, Jimmy, author. | Hembree, Michael, 1951- author. | Pearce, Al, 1942- author.
Title: NASCAR 75 years : the official history / Kelly Crandall, Jimmy Creed, Mike Hembree, and Al Pearce.
Other titles: NASCAR seventy-five years
Description: Beverly, MA : Motorbooks, 2022 | Includes index. | Summary: "Packed with evocative photography and a history written by some of the sport's most knowledgeable journalists, NASCAR 75 Years is the definitive story of America's favorite motorsport"-- Provided by publisher.
Identifiers: LCCN 2022042739 | ISBN 9780760380055 | ISBN 9780760380062 (ebook)
Subjects: LCSH: NASCAR (Association)--History. | Stock car racing--United States--History.
Classification: LCC GV1029.9.S74 .C69 2022 | DDC 796.720973--dc23/eng/20220930
LC record available at https://lccn.loc.gov/2022042739

Design and Page Layout: Cindy Samargia Laun
Cover Images: NASCAR

Printed in China

Contents

THE 1940s AND 1950s.......................8
Hot Wheels and Dirt Tracks

THE 1960s 38
Racing into the Superspeedway Era

THE 1970s...................66
Shifting into High Gear

THE 1980s...................96
Reaching the Threshold of Speed

THE 1990s...................124
Earnhardt and Gordon Drive the Sport Forward

THE 2000s 150
A New and Dark Millennium

THE 2010s...................178
Quintessential NASCAR

THE 2020s AND BEYOND........204
Next (Gen)eration

About the Writers...................218
Image Credits...................219
Index...................220

Gober Sosebee (50) in a 1949 Oldsmobile and Woodrow Wilson (12) in a 1949 Mercury lead the pack in a race run on the Daytona Beach & Road Course on July 10, 1949. It was the second race sponsored by the newly created stock car governing organization the National Association for Stock Car Auto Racing, or, as it is better known, NASCAR.

Chapter 1

THE 1940s AND 1950s

Hot Wheels and Dirt Tracks

By Mike Hembree

THE KID'S NAME was Richard Petty.

The date was June 19, 1949, and he was eleven years old. He wandered the grandstands at Charlotte Speedway with the curiosity one might expect of an eleven-year-old. And then some.

On the racetrack below, his father, Lee, was helping to pioneer a form of auto racing that the Petty family—in particular, that his kid, Richard—would come to dominate in the decades ahead. Over time, Richard's piano-key smile would spread across the continent.

Richard had ridden to the race—a 200-lap, 150-mile event on the three-quarter-mile dirt surface of the pock-marked track—with Lee and Maurice, Richard's brother. Lee, a thirty-five-year-old truck driver who had worked numerous jobs (including occasional transportation of illegal moonshine), was sailing around the dirt track like a madman, his 1948 Buick Roadmaster bouncing over the holes and banging into cars driven by others.

"I remember getting in the car and riding to Charlotte," Richard Petty said, more than seventy years later. "Daddy pulled it up to a Texaco station and put it up on the rack and changed the oil and greased it up, checked the air in the tires and took the muffler off."

It was ready to race.

No one—the father, the son, or the brother—could imagine on that day that all three of them eventually would wind up in the NASCAR Hall of Fame. In fact, none of them could imagine that there would be a NASCAR a year down the road.

It wasn't a grand start for Lee Petty. His tank of a race car broke a panhard bar and crashed hard. He finished seventeenth.

Richard doesn't remember much about the race, but he remembers his dad driving a flatbed truck from the Petty home in Randleman, North Carolina,

Three of the four cars that took part in one of the earliest drag races on the beach in January 1905. E. R. Thomas (6) and William K. Vanderbilt (1), both driving Mercedes, were challenged by Arthur MacDonald in a No. 5 Napier and Louis Ross in a Stanley Steamer (not pictured). Ross and the Stanley Steamer easily defeated the other trio of challengers.

to Charlotte the next day to haul the remains of the Buick to central North Carolina. "I don't know how Daddy explained it to the guys who owned the car," Richard said. Lee had "borrowed" the car to run the race—an audacious idea, but one no more audacious than the race itself.

Lee had driven the Buick from Randleman to the race site. With the car badly damaged, the family had to hitch a ride home with Lee's brother, Julian, for a reunion with Lee's wife, Elizabeth, who would have questions about the whole affair.

But Lee was not discouraged—the opposite, actually.

"The race paid $1,500 to win," Richard said. "That got Daddy's attention. He said, 'Hmmm.' He got home and told my mother, 'We could do this stuff.'"

A few days later, Lee, who had driven in some other races but none with the new-car smell, paid $990 for a 1949 Plymouth and eyed the rest of the schedule of NASCAR's first Cup (then Strictly Stock) season. "And that," Richard Petty said, "was the beginning of Petty Enterprises."

Lee, who set up his racing shop in an old reaper shed on the family property, drove six of the remaining seven races on the schedule, finishing second at Martinsville, Virginia, and North Wilkesboro, North Carolina, and winning at Pittsburgh, Pennsylvania.

Lee had found a way to put bread and meat on the family table, and William Henry Getty "Bill" France, the dreamer and schemer who had imagined that first race and what might follow, had discovered gold.

That crazy, dusty, dirty day on a beaten-up track surrounded by weather-worn wood fencing marked the first real mile in a journey that ultimately would revolutionize the still-young world of auto racing and make Bill France the king of a rising sun.

Spectators assist Frank Lockhart after he flipped his Stutz Blackhawk end over end into the surf while attempting a world land speed record run on Daytona Beach in February 1928. Quick action by the spectators saved Lockhart from drowning, and the only injury he suffered was a laceration on his hand. On Lockhart's next attempt, he crashed once again and lost his life.

Bill France Sr. with the Ford coupe he drove to a fifth-place finish in the 1936 Beach Road Race in Daytona Beach, Florida. France and other drivers raced along a course that combined the beachfront and a parallel paved stretch of Highway A1A, which was a two-lane road at the time. France qualified eighteenth with a speed of 63.02 mph.

A SUCCESSFUL OPENING

NASCAR, Bill France's fledgling racing organization, had been founded in December 1947 in Daytona Beach, Florida, but the Charlotte race in the closing year of the 1940s was its real birth. NASCAR had sanctioned Modified races—for modified prewar coupes that had seen better days—in 1948 and had other forms of motorsports in mind, but France's compass was centered on the idea of racing cars straight off the showroom floor. This, he said, would attract people because the cars they drove every day on country roads and highways would be thrown into close-contact competition while being driven by legitimate American daredevils.

The first Charlotte race would be the initial barometer of the concept. By any measure, it was a roaring success. Traffic backed up for miles around the tiny speedway, located near the present-day Charlotte airport. There are no reliable attendance figures from that long-ago afternoon. Estimates went as high as 20,000, but the time and place make it more likely that the crowd was between 10,000 and 15,000.

Several cars were destroyed during the race as the drivers tried to avoid bumps and holes and each other. At least seven cars were sidelined because of overheating. There were multiple crashes.

Glenn Dunaway finished first, but his car was disqualified by NASCAR officials because the rear end had been strengthened with powerful springs—not specifically to improve its racing posture but because it was a moonshine delivery vehicle in a former life. Dunaway's team challenged the decision in court, but NASCAR won the day, setting an important precedent—France could make and enforce his organization's rules.

Jim Roper, a Kansan who had learned about the race in a newspaper comic strip, finished second but was declared the winner. He had driven to Charlotte from Kansas in the 1949 Lincoln that won the race. He never won again; in fact, he raced only one other time in NASCAR before turning his attention to his horse farm.

Palm Beach millionaire and sportsman John Rutherford prefers the inside line as he leads a pack through the north turn in the No. 29 supercharged Auburn during the 1936 Beach Road Race staged in Daytona Beach, Florida.

The real winner on that June day was France.

A giant of a man, at well over 6 feet tall, France had relocated to Daytona Beach in 1934, moving south from Washington, D.C. A mechanic of sorts and a lover of fast cars, he immediately became interested in the timed speed runs and later the races taking place on the hard-packed oceanfront sand of Daytona Beach and nearby Ormond Beach.

Racing began on the Florida east coast in the early years of the twentieth century, as a collection of mostly rich adventurers hauled speed machines to the sandy shores of Ormond Beach and ran against the clock. They registered some crazily fast speeds—in the 300-mph range—and ran along the beach into the 1930s, when residential and commercial development made such activity increasingly difficult. The speed demons moved their fun to the Bonneville Salt Flats in Utah.

That left Daytona Beach without an annual speed carnival, and city leaders filled the void in 1936 by sponsoring a stock car race on a patched-together course combining the beachfront and a parallel paved stretch of Highway A1A. Drivers raced along the sand, then had to make a hard left turn onto A1A—at the time a two-lane road—before returning to the beach part of the course.

Although spectacular in its own way, the event lost money, and after a second try in 1937 the city moved on to other tourism-related ideas. France competed in the 1936 race, finishing fifth, and was convinced that racing along the beach had a future. He promoted a similar race in 1938 and, showing his talent for bringing in sponsors, awarded drivers with bottles of rum, boxes of cigars, and cases of motor oil.

France's first beach race was generally considered a success, and it gave him enough encouragement to push forward. Slowly but surely, he was moving from driving race cars to driving a sport. He had found his niche.

ABOVE: **The site where it all began: the Streamline Hotel in Daytona Beach. Preliminary meetings for the formation of NASCAR were held here in December 1947, with many of the negotiations for the formation of a national stock car racing governing body taking place on the rooftop of the Ebony Bar. After this meeting of drivers, promoters, track operators, and other racing stakeholders, NASCAR was incorporated the following year.**

ABOVE LEFT: **A group shot of the principals who gathered at the Streamline Hotel at the invitation of Bill France Sr. to discuss the formation of a national stock car racing organization in December 1947. Among the group were Louis "Red" Vogt, an Atlanta garage owner and racing mechanic; Joe Littlejohn, a driver and promoter from Spartanburg, South Carolina; Bill Tuthill, a promoter from New Rochelle, New York; and drivers such as Robert "Red" Byron and Marshall Teague.**

Lakewood Speedway was originally a 1-mile horse racing track built around the lake located at the Lakewood Fairgrounds just south of Atlanta. The first automobile races were held there in late 1917, and the track went on to become known as "the Indianapolis of the South" because it held an annual race of Indy cars.

DUST AND DIRT

A garrulous sort who tended to dominate any room he entered, France became fast friends with many of the drivers and hangers-on who converged on Daytona Beach for the beachfront races, giving him a foundation to expand his concept of motorsports competition to other venues.

Particularly across other Southern states, a raw form of stock car racing was being developed as men—and the occasional woman—toyed with their street cars and turned them into fast jalopies. They challenged each other on desolate highways and crude "racetracks" carved out of pastureland or backwoods acreage. Along the way, short oval tracks sprang up, and stock car racing moved into a period of ragged organization.

Drivers from those days battled awful conditions. "We raced at one track where it got so dusty that the only way you knew where to turn going into the turns was to count the telephone poles as you went by," said pioneer driver Jack Smith of Spartanburg, South Carolina.

As races got longer and drivers faced the reality of being on track for several hours, some mounted a rubber hose and a funnel on their floorboards so they could take care of bathroom business while racing. Buck Baker raced with a plow line from farming as a seat belt and wore the inner liner of a tank helmet for head protection. In a race on the Charlotte Speedway track, he used a pair of vise grips to "steer" after his steering wheel broke. Champion driver Herb Thomas remembered playing the radio in his car during races.

When the United States entered World War II in 1941, virtually all racing was shut down. France and other promoters who were trying to make something real out of a bare-bones idea, resumed racing after the war. In 1947, France announced the formation of the National Stock Car Racing Circuit, one of a handful of similar organizations popping up around the country. Fonty Flock, one of several members of the Flock family who would shine in racing's early years, won the 1947 seasonal championship and $1,000 prize money. There were a few other sanctioning groups scattered across the country, and the American Automobile Association ran events for stock-type cars in the 1930s.

The cars competing on France's circuit and on most other embryonic racing tours in the early years after the war were mostly rehabilitated prewar coupes. Car manufacturers had diverted their factories to the war effort and needed a few years to catch up with street vehicle production.

France was already looking to the future. With a keen eye on the way racing was evolving, and having concluded that the sport, which was being mismanaged by shady race promoters who often grabbed the purse money and ran, needed better structure, France made the move that made his name. He called a series of meetings in December 1947 in Daytona Beach for drivers, promoters, track operators, and others who might have a stake in the sport.

The men—and they were all men, unless we count the occasional woman invited to share a drink with the participants—gathered in the Ebony Bar atop the Streamline Hotel in downtown Daytona Beach. The meetings, which lasted four days, were advertised in racing publications as the annual convention of France's National Championship Stock Car Circuit. But he had much bigger

On July 10, 1949, Robert Nold "Red" Byron was the winner of the first-ever NASCAR–sanctioned national points race run on the Beach & Road Course in Daytona. Byron, shown here with the trophy, outran Marshall Teague and his own car owner, Raymond Parks, who finished third with relief from Bob Flock.

In the early years, the flagman was down on the track in the middle of all the racing action. Here Ed Samples takes the checkered flag, winning a Modified stock car race at Lakewood Speedway in Atlanta sometime in the late 1940s.

plans; he wanted to start a new organization that would bring in some of the racers and promoters who had been involved in rival groups, creating a big motorsports organization with national ambitions.

France's reputation attracted significant names to the meetings. Among the group were Louis "Red" Vogt, an Atlanta garage owner and racing mechanic; Joe Littlejohn, a driver and promoter from Spartanburg, South Carolina; Bill Tuthill, a New Rochelle, New York promoter; drivers Robert "Red"

Byron, Marshall Teague, Ed Samples, and Sam Packard, a Midget racer from Providence, Rhode Island.

Years later, Packard, who worked at a Daytona Beach service station owned by France after serving in the 82nd Airborne in World War II, defined the group as "Yankees and Southerners and bootleggers. But everybody went along pretty good with what needed to be done."

As the men gathered around tables in the bar, France began the meetings with a long speech outlining the current state of racing and proposing a new umbrella organization to develop standard rules and a national schedule. After hours of discussion and more than a few cocktails across four days, the organization had a framework and—finally—a name. Vogt is given credit for suggesting the NASCAR name, and the participants voted to accept it after originally choosing National Stock Car Racing Association.

To no one's surprise, France was elected NASCAR president. Two months later, on February 21, 1948, NASCAR was established as a privately owned corporation. The organization's first race—a 150-mile Modified event at Daytona Beach—was held six days earlier.

"On the outcome of his meeting and the decisions reached here rests the future of stock car racing," France had said in opening the meeting. His prediction bore fruit.

SHOWROOM TO SHOWDOWN

NASCAR was up and running. The first office was established in France's house on Goodall Avenue in Daytona Beach. The first NASCAR memberships were sold for $10 each and included a car decal and a membership card.

NASCAR was open to women drivers from its outset. Sara Christian competed in six of eight races in NASCAR's inaugural season in 1949 while Louise Smith took part in three. Christian ran just one other race in 1950 while Smith drove in a total of eleven races over the course of the 1949, 1950, and 1952 seasons. Smith is shown here with the 1947 Ford she wrecked in a race at Occoneechee Speedway in Hillsboro, North Carolina, on August 7, 1949. She finished twenty-seventh in a twenty-eight car field.

In a 1949 Plymouth, Glenn Dunnaway (49) battles the 1948 Buick of June Cleveland during a Grand National race at Charlotte Speedway on April 2, 1950. The race was won by Tim Flock, with Dunnaway finishing sixth and Cleveland seventeenth.

In 1948, NASCAR's first year, the organization sanctioned fifty-two races, opening doors for Modified competition across the country. But France had bigger fish to fry. With car builders ramping up production and Americans taking to the road in the newfound freedom of the postwar years, he wanted to put showroom-fresh sedans on race tracks—in part to give NASCAR something that other racing organizations lacked—and so he began planning for the first race. On February 20, 1949, France staged an experimental race for stock cars at Broward Speedway near West Palm Beach, Florida, and the results were encouraging.

Everything came together on the June day in Charlotte, a growing city that eventually would become a NASCAR capital. A band of road warriors, men who would form much of the pioneer class of Cup racing, rolled onto the track in hulking stock cars. Minor changes (headlights and bumpers were taped for protection, and metal plates were used to reinforce wheel strength on the rutted track) were allowed.

"The cars were pretty much just like they came from the dealers," said Tim Flock, one of the drivers and a future NASCAR champion. "No roll bars. No nothing. No one had ever run brand-new cars, and people came out just to see what was going to happen."

ABOVE: **NASCAR great Tim Flock with "Jocko Flocko," the rhesus monkey who was Flock's co-driver when he won a Cup Series race at Hickory Motor Speedway on May 16, 1953. The monkey was retired two weeks later at a race in Raleigh, North Carolina, when it pulled the device to allow Flock to observe the right front tire and was hit by a pebble. At the time, drivers used a device to lift the wheel well to observe tire wear. Flock had to make a pit stop to remove the monkey and finished third. (He likely would have won without the complication.)**

RIGHT: **Norm Nelson in a Chrysler (299) races with Speedy Thompson in a Ford (297) during the Cup Series race at Memphis-Arkansas Speedway on October 9, 1955. Thompson went on to win the event.**

France scheduled seven other Strictly Stock races that year. Oddly, in what would be labeled for years a Southern sport, two of the first season's races were held in Pennsylvania and another in New York.

Among the winners in that first abbreviated season was Virginian Curtis Turner, a sawmill operator who had his hands in a number of businesses but who had only two true loves: Racing and partying. With blue eyes and wavy brown hair, he was a racing star in the years before NASCAR. Driving on the ragged edge, he perfected the art of broadsliding through dirt-track turns, slinging the rear end of his car into the turn and letting the car settle into a straight line to tear down the backstretch. Turner's sidekick, Joe Weatherly, was another star of the 1950s and drew attention by racing in saddle Oxford shoes.

Turner won at treacherous Langhorne (Pennsylvania) Speedway in the first Cup season, conquering a tough track that claimed many lives over the years. In fact, the first two deaths in NASCAR-sanctioned events occurred at Langhorne. Larry Mann was killed September 14, 1952, and Frank Arford died in an accident while qualifying at the track June 20, 1953.

"Because the [Langhorne] track was round, you couldn't see very far ahead of you," said Rex White, the 1960 Cup champion. "If you suddenly ran up on cars, it was hard to dodge them. You were running pretty fast, so if you hit there was a lot of impact."

In racing's early years, cars had very few safety modifications, and accidents were sometimes fatal or resulted in gruesome injuries. Fire was a constant threat. Among others who died in the 1950s were Lou Figaro, John McVitty, Clint McHugh, Thomas Priddy, Bobby Myers, and Gwyn Staley.

SERIES GETS A SIGNATURE RACE

The biggest event of NASCAR's first decade occurred in the last year of the 1950s as founder Bill France Sr. ushered in what would become the sport's most important race—the Daytona 500.

The wildly fast 2.5-mile Daytona International Speedway track replaced a decade of racing on the beach-road course on Daytona Beach, Florida's oceanfront. The beach races, which tested drivers on a double course that included the sands of the beach and the parallel asphalt highway A1A, were popular, but continuing construction in the area made it clear motorsports competition there couldn't continue.

France had dreams of challenging Indianapolis Motor Speedway for speed and prominence, and DIS gave him his first big chance to score on a national level.

The first 500 did not disappoint. Cars reached speeds— Bob Welborn started on the pole at faster than 140 miles per hour—far faster than at any other stock car track, and drivers and mechanics marveled at what they considered the new "wide open spaces" of racing.

Incredibly, the 500 miles were recorded with no caution flags, and it became clear late in the afternoon that, barring incidents or mechanical problems, the race would be decided between Lee Petty and Johnny Beauchamp.

The two crossed the finish line side by side, with the lapped car of Joe Weatherly making the finish three-wide. Photographer T. Taylor Warren, whose classic photos would define NASCAR's early years, was in perfect position to record the finish. Beauchamp originally was declared the winner, but France decided to review film and still photographs of the finish and announced three days later that Petty had won. The delay earned France and his new speedway a long run of publicity and helped give the 500 an extra boost out of the gate.

Petty won $19,050, a staggering amount for the time. He and Beauchamp were the only drivers to complete the race's 200 laps. Fifty-nine drivers competed in the race, including Petty's son, Richard, who finished 57th after engine problems and won $100.

His earnings would multiply over the next decade, and he would win the 500 seven times.

Running three wide, Joe Weatherly (48), Lee Petty (42), and Johny Beauchamp (73) thrill fans at the inaugural Daytona 500 on February 22, 1959. Petty would go on to win. Beauchamp and Weatherly finished second and fifth, respectively.

Byron, a Virginia native who had won his first race competing against friends in a cow pasture, was the first Cup series champion. A flight engineer during World War II, he was wounded over the Aleutian Islands and wore a steel stirrup over his left leg while racing.

There were drivers who could have been NASCAR stars but didn't make it to France's big show. Lloyd Seay, one of the big guns of racing's early ragtag years and a winner at Atlanta's Lakewood Speedway in the 1930s, died at the age of twenty-one. He was shot in an argument over a delivery of sugar to a moonshine operation. Seay raced for Atlanta car owner Raymond Parks, a sharp dresser who brought stylishly painted cars to the track. More than a few drivers who succeeded in NASCAR's formative years learned how to drive fast cars skillfully while outrunning law-enforcement vehicles on twisty backroads as they made moonshine deliveries.

One of NASCAR's all-time greatest minds was rule-bender, car designer, and master mechanic Henry "Smokey" Yunick, seen here outside his Daytona Beach garage with the 1955 Oldsmobile owned by Ernest Woods and driven by Jim Paschal.

Drivers Speedy Thomas (M–1), Fred Fryar (492), and others streak past the roaring surf of the Atlantic Ocean in a Modified race in 1956.

Cotton Owens (6) leads Jack Smith (47) and Banjo Matthews (8) during the Cup Series race on the Daytona Beach & Road Course on February 17, 1957. Owens went on to win the event, the first of his nine career NASCAR wins.

SAND AND SURF

The Daytona beach-road course races continued, attracting bigger crowds, with NASCAR in charge and France wielding his promotional power. To discourage fans from trying to watch the races without paying, France put up signs on the grounds in the middle of the course warning of rattlesnakes.

The racing on the beach—the longest of several beach courses was 4.1 miles—remains legendary.

"The sand stayed wet all the time," remembered Joe Littlejohn, who drove in the early years but then spent most of his career promoting events and partnering with France. "You were always throwing it on the windshields of other cars. It would eventually sandblast the front end of the car. You couldn't see to drive the car home at night after the race. We used to run four, five, and six abreast on the beach section of the course. I've seen guys come out of the south turn late in the race with the tide coming in and slide out into the water."

Some beach races were shortened because of the tide. The rising Atlantic Ocean served as a significant deterrent (although several drivers reported edging over into the water to cool their tires).

The 1952 beach race marked the first appearance by an African American—Joie Ray—in a NASCAR-sanctioned race. He finished fifty-first. A few other Black drivers—notably Virginian Wendell Scott—would follow.

With seaside development putting pressure on the area that contained the beach-road racecourse, and with it becoming more difficult to close the main beach highway for racing, France realized early in the 1950s that it would be impossible to sustain beach racing. He began looking for an alternative, and in 1955 he started discussions with Daytona Beach officials about building a massive speedway west of town. Envious of the speeds and history of Indianapolis Motor Speedway and its fast, open-wheel cars, France wanted a stock car track that could challenge Indy for headlines.

THE FIRST PAVED RACEWAY

For its first two seasons, in the 1948 Modified division and in the inaugural year of Strictly Stock racing in 1949, NASCAR raced on earth—either the dirt of short tracks or the sand of the Daytona beach-road course.

Stock car racers had nothing that would remotely compare to the giant Indianapolis Motor Speedway, a 2-mile rectangular track that had hosted races since 1913 and had become the defining location for American motorsports.

Harold Brasington, a farmer from the Lowcountry of South Carolina, attended Indianapolis 500s in the 1930s and was impressed both by the competition and the crowds. He thought: Why couldn't the South and its racers have something similar?

Brasington boldly answered his own question by building Darlington Raceway in his own neighborhood. It was quite the task, one that Brasington approached with two hands and a bulldozer.

He reached an agreement—sealed only by a handshake, he said years later—with Darlington landowner Sherman Ramsey to build a track on Ramsey's property. Famously, the finished oval track would have a lopsided, egg-shaped look because Ramsey wanted Brasington to retain a small fishing pond on one end of the property.

"His burning desire was to foster competitive events and athleticism for average guys," said Harold Brasington II, the Darlington builder's grandson. "He was a star football and baseball player in high school. He kind of took that to racing. He drove some. He thought racing fostered that sort of 'Every guy can get out there and compete' idea. His interests were creating venues where people could get out and compete and see a variety of competitions."

Brasington said his grandfather also built bowling alleys, arcades, and other racetracks, including dragways, but Darlington Raceway would stand as his monument.

With investment from local businesspeople and a good eye for which pile of dirt should be placed in which location, Brasington carved the 1.25-mile track (it later was reconfigured to 1.366 miles) from Ramsey's property alongside South Carolina Highway 151. By the late summer of 1950, the track was ready for racing. For the first time, NASCAR drivers and their cars would compete on a 100 percent asphalt surface. More importantly, they would race for 500 miles, a brutal test for cars typically raced for 100 or 200 miles on 0.5-mile dirt tracks.

Contested on September 4, 1950, before a sellout crowd, the first Southern 500 was a marathon. Several drivers who participated described it as "total chaos."

A packed field of 75 cars—essentially double the grids of the modern era—started the race. Most fell behind the lead group very early. Buck Baker, Curtis Turner, and Jack Smith, future stars of the sport, crashed out of the event. Virtually every driver wrestled with tire problems, and most made repeated pit stops for fresh rubber. Some teams ran out of tires and sent crew members into the infield to remove tires from passenger vehicles to put on race cars.

In the end, the race win went to Johnny Mantz, ironically the slowest qualifier in the field. He ran steady and sure and benefited from using truck tires of a harder compound. He outran second-place Fireball Roberts by nine laps after 6 hours and 38 minutes of racing.

The race wasn't a classic as far as style, but it proved that NASCAR's drivers and cars could withstand long races, and it established Darlington Raceway as one of the sport's early capitals.

CURTIS TURNER IN PITS
DARLINGTON SPEEDWAY

The first Southern 500 at Darlington was contested on September 4, 1950, before a sellout crowd. Here Curtis Turner pits his Oldsmobile as Chuck Mahoney (77), Fonty Flock (47), Bill Rexford (59), and Herschel McGriff (52) fly past.

Convertible races were among the many kinds of races staged on the Beach & Road Course. Here Lee Petty (42) in a 1957 Oldsmobile is challenged by Possum Jones (48) driving a 1957 Chevy.

Work on Daytona International Speedway (DIS) began in the autumn of 1957. Midwesterner Paul Goldsmith, who had moved into stock car racing after success on fast motorcycles, won the last beach race in 1958, and the world's fastest stock car track opened with the first Daytona 500 in February 1959.

DIS, 2.5 miles long and high-banked, introduced NASCAR drivers to dramatically faster speeds and a new style of racing. Remarkably, the first 500 was completed without a caution flag, although the race ended in controversy. The checkered flag flew as three drivers—Lee Petty, Johnny Beauchamp, and Joe Weatherly (who had been lapped)—crossed the finish line three abreast. From one angle, it appeared that Beauchamp had finished first, and France declared him the winner. But, after three days of studying film and photographs (and gaining a ton of publicity because of the wait), France decided that Petty was slightly ahead and made him the winner of the first 500.

Drivers get ready to fire up their engines for a NASCAR Convertible Division race at Champion Speedway in Fayetteville, North Carolina, on March 10, 1957. Bob Welborn (49) started his Chevrolet from the pole, but it would be the driver on the outside pole, Glen Wood in his Ford (21), who would win the race.

A SHORT BUT SWEET STINT

Carl Kiekhaefer, one of the most successful team owners in NASCAR history, had a short but very productive time in the sport.

He entered teams at NASCAR's top level in 1955 and 1956, winning the championship in both seasons. Drivers Tim Flock and Buck Baker won those trophies. Then, as suddenly as he had appeared to start the 1955 season, Kiekhaefer vanished.

In only two years, however, the Wisconsin native had a major impact on NASCAR and built a template of sorts for future competitors. He concentrated on the "team" aspect of the sport, bringing a fleet of fine-tuned cars to each track and outfitting his crewmen in spotless uniforms, the first team owner to do so.

Kiekhaefer also scored another first. He used racing as a national advertising vehicle for Mercury outboard engines, one of his products. Signage shouting KIEKHAEFER OUTBOARDS was painted on the sides of the bright white Chrysler 300s raced by Kiekhaefer's drivers.

"Mr. Kiekhaefer was more or less a genius," said Flock, who won 18 races in 1955 in Kiekhaefer's cars. "His father started the Mercury outboard business, and he had thousands of outboard dealers across the country. He gave me every nickel I ever won in the cars. All he wanted was to advertise Mercury outboards."

Working for Kiekhaefer wasn't all peaches and cream, however. He made weird rules for his drivers, including demanding that they do not sleep with their wives the night before a race. To enforce that idea, he rented dozens of motel rooms at race sites so that the men and women could be separated easily.

"He would watch us all night to keep us apart," Flock said. "Things like that got worse and worse."

After Baker won the 1956 championship, Kiekhaefer, apparently not satisfied that he was getting a big enough return on investment in racing, dropped out of the sport for good.

Carl Kiekhaefer (left) chats with drivers (from left) Herb Thomas, Buck Baker, and Speedy Thompson.

The driver of this car in an April 14, 1957 race at Langhorne Speedway is Ralph Earnhardt, father of Dale Earnhardt Sr. and grandfather of Dale Earnhardt Jr. Ralph Earnhardt drove for Petty Enterprises in this race, and finished fourteenth despite a late-race crash. Langhorne Speedway was located near the borough of Langhorne, Pennsylvania, a northern suburb of Philadelphia.

Eventual winner Bob Welborn (No. 49) leads the pack alongside Curtis Turner (No. 26) during a NASCAR Convertible Division race at Asheville–Weaverville Speedway on June 2, 1957.

Paul Goldsmith smiles and waves after surviving the NASCAR Convertible Division race at North Wilkesboro Speedway on September 22, 1957. It was Goldsmith's only Convertible Division win out of the seven races he ran in 1956 and 1957.

On June 5, 1958, Junior Johnson (55) drove Paul Spaulding's 1957 Ford to victory in the NASCAR Cup Series race at Columbia Speedway in Cayce, South Carolina.

Richard Petty's cousin, Dale Inman, traveled to Daytona Beach with the Petty family that year—they stayed at the Sea Dip motel on the beach—and worked for the team. He later would become one of the sport's best crew chiefs, earning a place in the Hall of Fame.

"We came through the tunnel into the track that first day, and it was just amazing to see," Inman said. "It was the biggest thing we had seen in racing. We went right to work. So much of it was trial and error."

A year earlier, in an example of the lengths to which drivers and teams stretched their resources in NASCAR's first decade, Inman and Maurice Petty, Richard's brother, went on quite an adventure. With Lee Petty in contention for the 1958 series championship (which he eventually would win), he raced in Trenton, New Jersey, on a Friday and decided to run at Riverside, California, two days later to gain more championship points.

Lee flew to the West Coast. Getting the race car there became a task for Inman and Maurice. It wasn't unusual for participants to drive their race cars to race sites in NASCAR's first decade, but the Inman–Petty trip was a long, strange one.

"Maurice and I drove the car across the country," Inman said. "We carried jack stands and tires and stuff in the back seat. It was crazy. Maurice got stopped six times [by police], and I got stopped once. We didn't get any tickets."

In 1950, NASCAR racers saw the first glimmer of a new age of racing as they traveled to what was then a revolutionary track—Darlington Raceway. Builder Harold Brasington, a dreamer who had been to Indianapolis and envisioned a

Coming through Turn 1 on lap 136 of the September 1, 1958, Southern 500 at Darlington Raceway, pole-sitter Eddie Pagan hit the end of a steel guardrail and tumbled down the track embankment. Pagan escaped with very minor injuries. The remainder of the race was run with a large chunk of the guardrail missing.

Construction of the original drive-through tunnels used to reach the Daytona International Speedway infield took place in 1958. The tunnels, which are still in use today, had to be strapped to the ground to keep them stationary in their position at low sea level.

big track for the South, carved the 1.25-mile asphalt course from the sandy soil of Darlington, South Carolina, and NASCAR raced on a paved surface for the first time there in September 1950. The egg-shaped track—later reshaped to 1.366 miles—was "designed" in that fashion to save a fish pond on the property.

Darlington hosted the first Southern 500—tickets cost $5—September 4, 1950. Drivers arrived two weeks early for qualifying sessions. No one knew what to expect. What they got was 6 hours and 38 minutes of racing and an overflow of worn-out tires. During the race, teams ran out of tires and sent people into the infield to take tires from passenger vehicles to put on the race cars. Johnny Mantz, a successful Midget racer, was the slowest qualifier in the seventy-five-car field but won the race with better tire management.

NASCAR drivers had proved they could race 500 miles on a tough track. France had put his show on asphalt for the first time. And, in the track infield, a kid selling snow cones for 10 cents each was learning the ropes of running races. His name was Bill France Jr.

NASCAR DOES DETROIT

Doors continued to open for Bill France Sr. He was given the opportunity to sanction a 250-mile race at the Michigan State Fairgrounds to celebrate Detroit's 250th anniversary, August 12, 1951. This was a plum deal for France, in large part because it gave him new entry into the halls of Detroit-based car manufacturers. Many kingpins of the industry attended the race, which featured drivers Red Byron, Lee Petty, Curtis Turner, and Marshall Teague but was won in somewhat of an upset by Kentuckian Tommy Thompson, his only NASCAR victory.

France's growing ties to the car manufacturers and the fans' interest in this new form of racing led to the car builders having substantial involvement in the sport as early as midcentury. The Hudson Hornet was a favorite car of racers in the early 1950s, and Hudson developed what it called a "severe usage kit" to bolster the race cars' suspensions. By the mid–1950s, Detroit factories were advertising in periodicals when their cars won NASCAR events.

Chrysler jumped heavily into stock car racing, particularly with revolutionary team owner Carl Kiekhaefer, who entered NASCAR in the mid–1950s and won dozens of races and two championships with a new approach—team racing. He brought a fleet of Chryslers to NASCAR tracks, dressed his mechanics in clean white uniforms and ran his operation with the regimentation of a military operation. Driver Tim Flock won a title with Kiekhaefer but later left the team because he couldn't deal with the owner's demands, which included forcing drivers to sleep separately from their wives at race sites the night before events.

BELOW LEFT: **Bill France Sr. proudly surveys the construction of the 2.5-mile Daytona International Facility as it takes shape in 1959.**

BELOW RIGHT: **NASCAR great Jack Smith is ready to race in a Modified stock car at Daytona on February 22, 1959. Although he competed in a number of NASCAR Cup Series races, Smith concentrated primarily on Modified cars for most of the 1950s before becoming a top star on the Cup circuit, winning twenty-one times during his career.**

A packed house watches the early laps of the 1959 Daytona 500. Bill France Sr. realized his dream of having a stock car track to rival the Indianapolis Motor Speedway when Daytona opened on February 22, 1959.

Jack Smith, one of Kiekhaefer's drivers, said he was paid $1,100 per month and kept all money he won from race purses. That was a big difference from Smith's pre–NASCAR days, when he often would race seven or eight times a week at a series of short tracks, often in the same car. "You knew you had to finish that race and the one the next night or you weren't going to eat good that week," he said.

Some of the best performances of the 1950s were scored by Tim Flock (eighteen wins in 1955), Buck Baker (fourteen in 1956), and Herb Thomas (twelve in both 1953 and 1954).

Two of the sport's giants emerged in the second half of the 1950s. Fireball Roberts and Junior Johnson combined to score thirty-six victories in the final five years of the decade.

Richard Petty, restless to join his father on the track, made his first Cup start July 18, 1958, in Toronto, Canada. He finished seventeenth in a field of nineteen. The poor result didn't dominate the day for the Petty family, because Lee Petty won.

The Petty racing machine rolled on.

Johnny Beauchamp stands in victory lane in what he thought was his win after the Daytona 500 at the Daytona International Speedway on February 22, 1959. Sixty-one hours later, a photo-finish was declared and Lee Petty was awarded the trophy over Beauchamp.

In a Ford Thunderbird, Tom Pistone (59) leads Rex White (4) on the high banks of Daytona International Speedway during the first Daytona 500 on February 22, 1959. Curtis Turner's Ford Thunderbird (41) races on the apron. Pistone finished third in the race, White finished tenth, and Turner finished twenty-ninth in the thirty-eight-car field.

Petty Enterprises would become one of the foundational teams of young NASCAR. "Daddy's decision to go racing worked," Richard said. "It worked for the family. It's still working. We're still living off that decision he made in 1949—the whole Petty crowd and thousands of people who worked with us or for us. No telling how many people were influenced by that decision."

Others who eventually became the other pillars of the sport were the Wood Brothers, based in Stuart, Virginia; Bud Moore Engineering, in Spartanburg, South Carolina; and Junior Johnson and Associates, in Ingle Hollow, North Carolina.

In his Ford Thunderbird, Curtis Turner leads the Chevrolet of Buck Baker during the Rebel 300 NASCAR Convertible Series race at Darlington Raceway on May 9, 1959.

LEE PETTY
(1954, 1958, 1959)

HERB THOMAS
(1951, 1953)

TIM FLOCK
(1952, 1955)

CHAMPS

Lee was the patriarch of the Petty racing dynasty, which eventually included his son Richard, grandson Kyle, and great-grandson Adam. The team Lee started in a small reaper shed on his North Carolina farm became one of the greatest motorsports operations in the country. He raced in NASCAR's first Strictly Stock race, flipping a huge Buick. Petty learned quickly and was practically fearless as he powered his way to 54 race wins, including the first Daytona 500, and three championships.

Thomas was the personification of the early NASCAR racer. A dirt farmer who saw a race and figured he could drive fast cars as well as anyone else, he jumped into the sport in its early days and quickly became a force. Thomas totaled 48 Cup wins, was the first driver to win two championships, and the first to win the Southern 500, a truly punishing race in the 1950s, three times.

Flock was the star in a family of racers. A pioneer of stock car racing, he drove in the first Strictly Stock race in 1949 and steadily built a reputation as one of the sport's best. "It was dog-eat-dog back in those days," he said. "All we were worried about was making enough money to take home to feed the kids." He won $3,000 for the seasonal championship in 1952.

BUCK BAKER
(1956, 1957)

RED BYRON
(1949)

BILL REXFORD
(1950)

Baker was the prototypical Southern stock car racer—fast, tough and stubborn. He often talked of being in postrace pit-road altercations that lasted longer than the race. His persistence led to one of the sport's best careers—46 race wins and back-to-back championships. Baker raced for a long list of team owners, evidence that his skills attracted attention across a broad range of NASCAR regulars. In the final year of his career, at the age of 57, he finished sixth at Darlington.

Byron will forever be honored as the first champion in what would become NASCAR's Cup Series. That title came a few years after Byron's service in World War II. A flight engineer, he suffered critical injuries when his plane was shot down and was able to return to racing postwar only after his injured left leg was clamped to the clutch. Byron is featured in an iconic NASCAR photograph from those years, his uniform and face covered in dirt after another successful run.

Rexford, a 23-year-old New York native, edged Fireball Roberts to win the 1950 Cup championship. During that season, Rexford scored his only series victory, leading 80 laps to win on a half-mile dirt track in Canfield, Ohio. Rexford drove in 17 of the series' 19 races in the division's second year, scoring 11 top tens. He retired from racing a few years later, becoming one of the sport's more obscure champions.

Fred Lorenzen takes the checkered flag at the 1964 Atlanta 500 after leading 206 of 334 laps. Lorenzen's Hollywood looks and aggressive driving style made him a fan favorite. He was among a group of notable drivers who retired in the 1960s, including Junior Johnson and Ned Jarrett. Lorenzen made a brief comeback attempt in 1970.

Chapter 2

THE 1960s

Racing into the Superspeedway Era

By Mike Hembree

THE 1960s WAS a decade of spectacular growth for NASCAR—growth in attendance and attention but most notably in landscape.

The trend began in the late 1950s with the construction and opening of Daytona International Speedway, the giant 2.5-mile track that would redefine NASCAR and launch a new age of speed. The clear attraction of bigger, faster speedways led to others popping up across the country.

A few months after the first Daytona 500 in February 1959, construction began on Charlotte Motor Speedway in Concord, North Carolina. Driver Curtis Turner and promoter Bruton Smith, men who ultimately would play oversized roles in the history of stock car racing, partnered on the track, which opened in 1960 under dark shadows of financial trouble because of construction issues.

Two states away, Atlanta International Raceway (now Atlanta Motor Speedway) opened in July 1960. On the other coast, Marchbanks Speedway opened that same year in Hanford, California. Bristol International Raceway (now Bristol Motor Speedway) came along in eastern Tennessee in 1961, followed by North Carolina Motor Speedway in Rockingham in 1965. Alabama International Motor Speedway (now Talladega Superspeedway), Michigan International Speedway, and Texas World Speedway hosted their first Cup races in 1969. Dover International Speedway in Delaware ran its first Cup race July 6, 1969 (remarkably, only two days after Cup drivers had competed in the annual summer race at Daytona Beach). Pocono Raceway opened in the Pocono Mountains of Pennsylvania in 1969 but didn't appear on the Cup schedule until 1974.

The doors were swinging wide for NASCAR to move away from the tiny tracks upon which the sport's foundation had been built, but that movement wouldn't assume full flower until the early 1970s.

An aerial view of a portion of the Charlotte Motor Speedway during its inaugural race, the World 600 on June 19, 1960. Hastily constructed under tight deadlines, the racing surface broke up badly, causing chunks of asphalt to kick up and damage race cars. Conditions were serious enough that many drivers added screens to the front of their cars in an attempt to prevent damage.

TOP: **Richard Petty (right) and the rest of the field prepare to start a race at Orange Speedway in Hillsborough, North Carolina, on September 18, 1960. It was his third win of the 200 Petty would go on to earn in his career.**

LEFT: **Richard Petty leads the pack in a Plymouth during one of the two races run at Martinsville Speedway in 1960. Petty won the 1960 Virginia 500, one of his fifteen career Cup Series wins at NASCAR's shortest venue.**

ABOVE: **Junior Johnson wrecked his primary car, a 1961 Pontiac, in his qualifying race for the 1961 Daytona 500, and was forced to run a backup 1960 model. He finished forty-seven.**

RIGHT: **Lee Petty and Johnny Beauchamp (No. 73) sail over the Turn 4 railing of Daytona International Speedway after tangling on lap thirty-seven of the second qualifier race for the 1961 Daytona 500. Both cars eventually ended up outside the speedway. This was an unexpected twist, as both drivers had been involved in the famous photo finish at the first Daytona 500 in 1959.**

SUPERSTARS ARRIVE

The 1960s saw the arrival of two drivers who would become fierce rivals as they pushed the sport to new heights. Richard Petty won the Cup championship in 1964 and 1967, and David Pearson won the title in 1966 (with team owner Cotton Owens), 1968 and 1969 (with the legendary Holman-Moody Ford operation, a Detroit mainstay for many years). Both drivers built huge fan bases as NASCAR dominated the sports scene across the Southeast on most Sundays and, with the opening of new speedways scattered across the country, spread its reach into new frontiers.

The decade was filled with other names that would make headlines: Mario Andretti, Wendell Scott, Tiny Lund, Ned Jarrett, Cale Yarborough, Junior Johnson, Fireball Roberts, Fred Lorenzen, LeeRoy Yarbrough, and, perhaps most surprisingly, Richard Brickhouse.

The 1960s era of auto racing was also hammered by death and controversy. A string of NASCAR drivers, including stars Fireball Roberts and Joe Weatherly, died during the 1960s, prompting a revolution in safety advances. The most famous confrontation between drivers and officials in the history of the sport occurred in 1969 at the new Alabama International Motor Speedway, where most of NASCAR's leading drivers boycotted the track's opening race because of concerns over tire reliability.

DALE INMAN

t came as a surprise to virtually no one when Dale Inman was chosen as the first crew chief to be named to the NASCAR Hall of Fame.

Inman's selection to the hall's 2012 class came after a career that included a record 193 victories and a record eight championships.

Seven of those titles were won with Inman leading the Petty Enterprises team and driver Richard Petty, his cousin. Inman and Petty grew up together, riding bicycles near their rural North Carolina homes and playing football together in high school. Inman began traveling with the Pettys to races and helping at the team shop in Level Cross, and soon he became an invaluable member of the team.

Petty won championships in 1964, 1967, 1971, 1972, 1974, 1975, and 1979, all with Inman in charge of the pit crew and the in-shop mechanics. They built the template for a successful stock car team, dominating the sport with 27 victories, including 10 consecutive, on the way to a second championship in 1967. The blue Plymouth Petty drove to those victories eventually wound up in the Hall of Fame.

In the 1981 Daytona 500, Inman made a critical late-race decision, bringing Petty into the team pit for fuel only and gambling that their tires would last the rest of the way. Petty rolled on to his seventh 500 victory.

Inman was very emotional in Daytona's victory lane. Soon the sport understood the reason. Inman left the team to pursue other interests, later winning an eighth championship (in 1984) with driver Terry Labonte.

Inman returned to the Petty fold in 1986 and worked with the team as a consultant for many years afterward.

Dale Inman (left) confers with Richard Petty prior to the Macon 300 on June 6, 1967.

HEMI ENGINE

The 1963 Daytona 500 ended with Ford drivers crossing the finish line in the first five positions—winner Tiny Lund, Fred Lorenzen, Ned Jarrett, Nelson Stacy, and Dan Gurney. The top Plymouth driver—Richard Petty—limped home in sixth, two laps behind.

In a race that rapidly was becoming the stock car world's most important, this simply would not do. The powers-that-be at Chrysler vowed Ford products would not repeat such a runaway.

And they were right. Chrysler teams showed up at Daytona a year later with one of the marvels of auto racing history—the Chrysler Hemispherical Combustion Chamber Maximum Performance engine. Nobody could remember all that, so it became known as the Hemi.

The new powerplant had been proven in secret runs at a high-performance test track in Texas. Rarely has such a racing technological advancement had such a huge impact. A variety of the Hemi had been raced in the 1950s, but this new bolt came out of the blue. It was a monster. It even looked mean under the hood. Even today, engine builders talk about it with a certain sense of awe.

Its crazy impact could be seen in the difference between Richard Petty's Daytona performance from 1963 to 1964. In 1963, his qualifying speed was 154.785 mph. Fast forward a year later, and with 426-cubic-inch Hemi power boosting his Plymouth, Petty qualified at 174.418—a staggering difference of almost 20 mph.

Inside Daytona's garage area, Ford teams saw the future and realized it was dark, indeed.

Petty put a big stamp of approval on the new engine on race day, leading 184 of the Daytona 500's 200 laps and scoring the first of his seven wins in the race. He was the only driver on the lead lap at the finish, but two other Plymouth drivers—Jimmy Pardue and Paul Goldsmith—followed him home in second and third. It was a big flip of the script from the previous February.

The record speeds were a bit chilling. Petty, no shrinking violet on track, said he had to "stay right with the car every second."

Richard Petty pits during the Daytona 500 on February 23, 1964. Petty used the new Chrysler Hemi engine to rout the Daytona 500 field. His factory teammates, Jimmy Pardue and Paul Goldsmith, held down second and third places.

The relationships between NASCAR, its teams, and the Detroit factories was unsettled throughout most of the 1960s. The manufacturers officially had pulled out of racing in 1957 when the Automobile Manufacturers Association, made up of representatives from each factory, recommended a retreat from all forms of motorsports. In 1955, eighty-three spectators had been killed during the 24 hours of Le Mans when a car sailed into a fan area. The AMA decided, at least in public, to disassociate itself from speed and horsepower and to concentrate on safety.

But car sales were often directly linked to success on speedways during that period, and the car builders were in and out of racing over much of the next decade, often aiding NASCAR teams with assistance "under the table." The factories also rode an uneasy path in relationships with NASCAR, arguing over rule changes and occasionally boycotting races and seasons when rules seemed to bend toward one car make or another.

The 1960s also saw a sea change in car preparation as teams began the move from racing cars built by Detroit manufacturers to running cars that were purpose-built for competition.

"It was probably in 1963 when we started building cars from the ground up," said two-time champion Ned Jarrett. "Up until then you were taking a car off the showroom floor and building a race car out of it. The change had us starting with a chassis and going from there. We started making special chassis parts as opposed to welding to reinforce. We started making special spindles that were larger and stronger."

Wendell Scott (34) leads Maurice Petty (43) and Rex White (4) during a Cup Series race at Orange Speedway in Hillsboro, North Carolina, on April 2, 1961. It was only the second Cup Series start in Scott's thirteen-year career, and he finished thirteenth.

Action during the first Cup Series race run at Bristol International Speedway, the 1961 Volunteer 500 on July 30. In a 1960 Ford, Curtis Crider (62) leads the 1960 Chevrolet of Tommy Wells (39), the 1960 Oldsmobile of Reb Wickersham (33), the 1960 Chevrolet of Wendell Scott (34), and others early in the race. Jack Smith won the race by lapping the entire field twice.

RICHARD PETTY RULES DAYTONA

As NASCAR grew, Richard Petty took the racing baton from his championship father, Lee, for Petty Enterprises and made tiny Randleman, North Carolina, an international motorsports capital.

As Daytona International Speedway gathered steam as a major motorsports attraction, Richard and his team put their stamp on Daytona. The track and the driver sort of grew up together, even as speeds over the 2.5 miles accelerated with each race. At Daytona, driver Cale Yarborough said, "You don't drive, you aim."

Richard won the 1964 500 in dominating fashion, riding behind the new and powerful Chrysler 426-cubic-inch Hemi engine, a powerplant that would create turmoil in NASCAR garages because of its strength.

LEFT: **Cale Yarborough in his driver's suit prior to the 1962 Daytona 500. It was the first of twenty-seven Daytona 500s Yarborough ran in his Hall of Fame career.**

BELOW: **Cale Yarborough started twenty-first in the 1962 Daytona 500 but finished last in the forty-eight-car field, running just four laps before electrical failure took him out of the race.**

The Ford of Johnny Allen sails over the railing on lap forty-four of the Dixie 400 Cup race at Atlanta Motor Speedway on June 30, 1963. The engine of Allen's car was ripped from its frame and landed some 100 feet from the rest of the car. Despite the severity of the crash, Allen suffered only a small cut on his nose.

ANDRETTI MAKES A VISIT

A year later, the Daytona 500 had a surprise winner. Mario Andretti, who dipped into NASCAR racing occasionally but is much more widely known for IndyCar and Formula 1 success, tackled Daytona in a Holman–Moody Ford. Andretti had no plans to become a NASCAR regular, but he wanted to leave his mark on the race that rapidly was becoming the biggest star in the stock car constellation. He ran a different line from the regulars, letting the car's rear end slide in the corners, and led 112 of the 200 laps, including the final thirty-three, to score his only win in NASCAR. Andretti raced fourteen times in the Cup over a four-year period.

It's generally accepted sports gospel that all records are made to be broken, but one of Richard's seems certain to stand the test of time. In his wildly successful 1967 championship season, Petty won twenty-seven races. Incredibly, he won ten in a row.

The streak, recorded in a single blue Plymouth with a white No. 43 on each side, started August 12 and ran through October 1. Richard won at Winston-Salem, North Carolina; Columbia, South Carolina; Savannah, Georgia; Darlington, South Carolina; Hickory, North Carolina; Richmond, Virginia; Beltsville, Maryland; Hillsborough, North Carolina; Martinsville, Virginia; and North Wilkesboro, North Carolina. When Petty arrived in the North Wilkesboro press box for the winner's interview after ten in a row, he said, "How about me interviewing you guys today? I don't have much to say that I haven't already said."

Dewayne Louis "Tiny" Lund (21) won the 1963 Daytona 500 in storybook fashion. Lund was chosen to take the place of the Wood Brothers' regular driver, Marvin Panch, after he helped free Panch from a burning, overturned sports car when he had crashed earlier in the month during practice for the Daytona Continental. Lund saved Panch's life, and Panch repaid him by asking the Wood Brothers to put Lund in the car for the Great American Race and the great American finish.

RIGHT: **Wendell Scott, who raced out of Danville, Virginia, made 495 career Cup Series starts and recorded one win, twenty top-five finishes, and 147 top-ten finishes.**

BELOW: **Prior to the Cup Series Coke Zero Sugar 400 at Daytona International Speedway on August 28, 2021, NASCAR President Steve Phelps presents the family of NASCAR Hall of Fame driver Wendell Scott with a trophy for the 1963 Jacksonville 200 win. Scott was not announced as the race winner that day in Jacksonville. Second-place driver Buck Baker was initially declared the winner, but race officials discovered 2 hours later that Scott had not only won, but had been two laps in front of the rest of the field. NASCAR awarded Scott the win two years later, but his family never received the trophy he had earned until 2021—nearly fifty-eight years after the race, and thirty-one years after Scott had died.**

An accident and engine trouble ended the Petty streak the next week at Charlotte Motor Speedway, but his army of fans grew exponentially, and more than a few spectator cars showed up at race tracks with "Petty for President" bumper stickers.

PIONEERS DRIVE AWAY

Richard Petty's star was rising as some of NASCAR's biggest names drove toward the exits. Junior Johnson, Ned Jarrett, Fred Lorenzen, and Marvin Panch retired in the middle of the decade, and Fireball Roberts and Joe Weatherly died in accidents. Lorenzen, whose Hollywood looks and aggressive driving style made him a fan favorite, retired in 1967 but returned three years later for a brief and unsuccessful second stint. He scored six wins in 1963 and became the first NASCAR driver to win more than $100,000 in a season.

Three drivers edged into stardom in the second half of the decade. Bobby Allison, who built a strong racing résumé in Florida but settled in Alabama and became the leader of the Alabama Gang of racers, won three races in 1966 and doubled that total the next year. He became a weekly foil for Petty, the man of the moment, and they had numerous on-track encounters. Cale Yarborough rolled out of Lowcountry, South Carolina, and soon became a victory threat, winning six races with the Wood Brothers in 1968. LeeRoy Yarbrough, whose career would be a fast comet across the skies before health issues intervened, won seven times in 1969 as he became one of the most feared racers on big tracks.

In 1961, a driver arrived on the NASCAR scene who would change the face of the sport—literally. Wendell Scott, a Black driver who had had success on short tracks in and around his home state of Virginia, raced in Cup for the first time March 4, 1961, at the Piedmont Interstate Fairgrounds dirt track in Spartanburg, South Carolina. Several other Black drivers had run a few races in NASCAR, but Scott was the first to become a semiregular on the tour. Poorly funded and doing most of the work on his cars himself, Scott raced against the wind, dealing with the discrimination of the time and hearing derisive calls from the grandstands.

Scott would be at the center of one of the biggest controversies in NASCAR history. On December 1, 1963, at a now-forgotten short track near Jacksonville, Florida, Scott became the first African American driver to win a Cup race. He didn't get rewarded immediately for that accomplishment, however, because officials apparently were concerned about a Black man sharing victory lane with a white woman serving as race queen. Veteran Buck Baker was declared the race winner.

After a recheck of scorecards, Scott was named the winner, but he had already left the track. He received the winner's paycheck days later, but the original winner's trophy was never awarded to him. Decades later, NASCAR, which had acknowledged its mistake, presented a duplicate trophy to members of Scott's family. Wendell Scott retired in 1973, with that unusual day in Florida his only Cup success.

JUNIOR JOHNSON IS A STAR

Of all the things that gave NASCAR higher visibility in the 1960s, one of the most unusual was a magazine article. Noted writer and reporter Tom Wolfe, whose books became frequent residents of bestseller lists, ventured to the Brushy Mountains of North Carolina to write an *Esquire* magazine article on Junior Johnson, then one of racing's stars. Wolfe documented Johnson's remarkable rise from country boy and moonshiner to racing champion while also painting a broad and colorful picture of stock car racing and its fandom. The article, which appeared in 1965, is considered one of the best long-form magazine stories ever published, and it gave NASCAR a significant shot of publicity. Johnson called the story a great honor but emphasized that, "I was still Junior. And that's who I'll be until the day I die."

With attendance figures showing growth and new speedways joining NASCAR's list, television executives began exploring this wild new world of sports. The first live network television coverage of Cup racing occurred January 31, 1960, as CBS Sports covered two qualifying races for the Daytona 500. In 1961, ABC televised parts of the summer race at Daytona, and that—joining a race in progress and broadcasting it until the finish—became somewhat of a template for early television coverage of NASCAR. The major networks were hesitant to devote hours of coverage to races that stretched past 4 hours. The first flag-to-flag live coverage of a Cup race wouldn't happen until 1971.

Fireball Roberts generally is recognized as NASCAR's first superstar racer, and he stood out in some of those early television days. Smart, fearless, and handsome, Roberts took to racing's new faster tracks like a tiger to meat. He logged thirty-two Cup victories, much of his success being scored with legendary mechanic Smokey Yunick, whose work was both innovative and suspicious.

Entering the 1964 season, Roberts, thirty-five, had decided to retire after running a few more major races. He had agreed to become the spokesman for a beer brand and was planning his postracing life.

BELOW LEFT: **Ray Fox entered three Chevrolets in the National 500 NASCAR Cup race at Charlotte Motor Speedway. Junior Johnson (3) went on to win the race, while Jim Paschal (03) and Buck Baker (33) both dropped out with mechanical problems.**

BELOW RIGHT: **Edward Glenn "Fireball" Roberts (22) in a Ford, Rex White (4) in a Mercury, and Marvin Panch (21) and Ned Jarrett (11) in Fords prepare along with the rest of the field for the start of the September 22, 1963, Old Dominion 500 Cup Series race at Martinsville Speedway.**

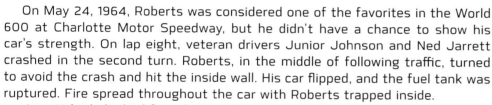

ABOVE: **Edward Glenn "Fireball" Roberts was one of NASCAR's first superstars, posting thirty-two of his thirty-three Cup Series victories between 1956 and early 1964. Roberts died on July 2, 1964, from burns sustained in a fiery crash on lap seven of the World 600 at Charlotte Motor Speedway.**

LEFT: **A dapper Ned Jarrett (right) talks with fellow driver Fred Lorenzen before a mid-1960s NASCAR race. Together, the pair won seventy-six NASCAR Cup races during their careers, and Jarrett won the 1961 NASCAR championship.**

On May 24, 1964, Roberts was considered one of the favorites in the World 600 at Charlotte Motor Speedway, but he didn't have a chance to show his car's strength. On lap eight, veteran drivers Junior Johnson and Ned Jarrett crashed in the second turn. Roberts, in the middle of following traffic, turned to avoid the crash and hit the inside wall. His car flipped, and the fuel tank was ruptured. Fire spread throughout the car with Roberts trapped inside.

Jarrett had climbed from his crashed car and heard Roberts screaming for help. "Oh, my God, Ned, help me. I'm on fire," Roberts yelled, words that Jarrett would remember again and again through the years. Jarrett helped Roberts remove his burned uniform.

Rushed to a nearby hospital, Roberts suffered from burns over much of his body. He rallied a few times over the next several weeks, but pneumonia and a blood infection weakened his body, and he died July 2. He was laid to rest in a Daytona Beach cemetery within earshot of the speedway.

Two-time Cup champion Joe Weatherly, one of Roberts' best friends, had died January 19, 1964, in a vicious crash at Riverside International Raceway in California. The year was a dark one for racing, as stock car drivers Billy Wade, Jimmy Pardue, Roberts, Weatherly, and IndyCar drivers Eddie Sachs and Dave MacDonald died in crashes. Buren Skeen (1965), Harold Kite (1965), and Billy Foster (1967) also died in accidents.

After Roberts' death, the sport responded with safety advances, including the development of a rubber fuel cell to guard against gasoline fires, flameproof driver uniforms, and fire extinguishers to mount inside cars. Goodyear Tire and Rubber Co. developed an inner liner to make racing tires stronger and safer.

"Before the fireproof uniforms, when we ran on superspeedways, we were required to bring whatever clothing we were going to wear in the race two days

During the 1966 Dixie 400 at Atlanta Motor Speedway on August 7, Fred Lorenzen drove the Junior Johnson-owned No. 26 Ford, which remains one of the most widely discussed vehicles in Cup Series history because it was illegal and NASCAR officials knew it before the race. NASCAR allowed this illegal car to run in just one race in an attempt to bring up attendance, which had suffered due to a Ford boycott of Cup Series racing that year. The car was referred to as "The Yellow Banana," "Junior's Joke," and "The Magnafluxed Monster." Lorenzen finished twenty-third.

The scoreboard shows Richard Petty leading one of the two Cup Series races run at Martinsville Speedway in 1967. Not only did Petty lead both the Virginia 500 and the Old Dominion 500, but he won both as well. Petty won just about everything in 1967: he won a NASCAR record of twenty-seven races of the forty-nine races run while also earning the second of his seven career championship victories.

before the race," Jarrett remembered. "NASCAR would have a boiling solution of boric acid and other ingredients that would flameproof the clothes. You'd hang them on a fence to dry. They looked terrible, but you could put a blowtorch to them and they wouldn't catch fire. Fireball was allergic to that solution. I believe to this day if he had had a flameproof uniform he'd still be here."

TROUBLE AT TALLADEGA

Richard Brickhouse, a relatively unknown driver from Rocky Point, North Carolina, became the answer to a NASCAR trivia question in 1969 when the giant new Alabama International Motor Speedway opened its gates for racing in what became a calamitous week in September. NASCAR founder Bill France Sr. had built the 2.66-mile, high-banked track on the site of a former airport in eastern Alabama with the goal of producing speeds faster than its sister track in Daytona Beach, Florida. That goal was accomplished, but not without major controversy.

Reports from early rounds of testing on the track surface indicated that tires were blistering. News of that sort spreads rapidly through the driver–team community, and competitors arrived at the track for Talladega 500 preliminaries with more than the usual level of concern.

Charlie Glotzbach, a popular driver known for a hard-charging style, ran 199.466 mph in qualifying, and red flags flew up across the garage area. Glotzbach and Donnie Allison were assigned to run tire tests on the track Friday, and troubles continued. Firestone, then competing with Goodyear in the NASCAR tire market, withdrew its tires from the race after those runs.

On Saturday, the day before the race, the new Professional Drivers' Association, which included most of the leading drivers, voted to boycott the race because of safety issues, suggesting that the race be postponed until better tires could be produced.

LEFT: **Owner Clay Earles began the tradition of presenting a grandfather clock to each Martinsville Speedway winner in 1964, and Richard Petty collected a record number of twelve. Here Earles presents Petty with a clock following one of his two victories at the track in 1967.**

RIGHT: **Bill France (second from right) watches as dignitaries break ground on what would become the 2.66-mile Alabama International Motor Speedway on May 23, 1968. Built on the site of a former military airfield, the track is now known as the Talladega Superspeedway.**

TROUBLE AT TALLADEGA'S FIRST RACE

The 1960s roared to an end with NASCAR on the rise nationally and Bill France Sr. eagerly anticipating the opening of his huge new speedway in Talladega, Alabama. The track, then known as Alabama International Motor Speedway (now Talladega Superspeedway), was high-banked and imposing. At 2.66 miles, it was one of the biggest tracks in the auto racing world, and it was designed to be the fastest closed course ever built.

Unfortunately, the track's life began in chaos.

Tire tests on the new surface indicated speeds would be in the 200-mph range, but there also were issues with tires. Drivers at the tests were concerned that the tire compounds couldn't handle the high speeds.

As the September 14, 1969, opener approached, the Talladega tire situation and other matters led some drivers to gather for a secret meeting. That session resulted in the formation of the Professional Drivers Association. Richard Petty was elected president. The idea was to give the drivers a collective voice in discussions with NASCAR, but it was a concept that didn't impress France Sr., who was adamantly opposed to unions and similar organizations.

When teams arrived at Talladega for practice runs leading to the Sunday race, the PDA faced its first big test. Tires failed on several cars in the 190-mph range, and drivers encouraged France to postpone the race until tiremakers Firestone and Goodyear could develop stronger compounds. France, who couldn't live with the thought of his sparkling new racetrack being stained by such a postponement refused, suggesting that drivers slow to a safe speed.

Intentionally driving slower wasn't exactly a key drivers' goal

Firestone eventually pulled out of the race. Goodyea remained. France, a former driver, eventually ran laps or the track to certify its safety, although his speeds didn't approach the high numbers.

Dissatisfied, most of the sports' leading drivers left the track on Saturday, creating the odd sight of team trucks traveling away from the speedway even as fans drove in.

Defiant, France raced on. He held the Talladega 500 on Sunday, filling out the field with cars from a Saturday lower-division race. Richard Brickhouse and a few othe Cup regulars participated, and Brickhouse took the lead for good with 11 laps remaining. It would be his only Cup victory, and he steadily faded into the mists of history There were no serious incidents, in part because NASCAR slowed the pace of the race with strategically placed caution flags.

Tire technology eventually caught up with Talladega speeds and the track became one of the circuit's most popular.

Richard Brickhouse (99) claimed his only Cup victory at 1969's inaugural Talladega 500. Dissatisfied with track safety, most of the leading drivers pulled out of the event the day before the race.

TOP: **Workers pour concrete to build the outside retaining wall in the tri-oval area of the Alabama International Motor Speedway.**

ABOVE: **A closer view of a packing machine as it prepares one of Talladega's 33-degree banked turns for the asphalt racing surface to be put down.**

The 33-degree banking in Talladega's turns made it too steep for construction machinery to operate normally. Here a packing machine is secured to a bulldozer located at the top of the bank so the foundation can be packed before the asphalt is laid down.

Bill France inspects some of the material being used to build the 2.66-mile Alabama International Motor Speedway in Talladega, Alabama.

France was livid. He declared that the race would be run regardless and turned a few laps in a race car himself to prove that the tires were ok. Nevertheless, thirty of the sport's top drivers left the track Saturday.

"We disagreed and never came to any kind of meeting of the minds," said driver Bobby Allison. "I felt like it was wrong to race, and I was one of the ones that left. I went to the house. I felt very, very justified in what I had done, and I felt that the thing shouldn't have been run on that day but that the fans should have gotten to see a Winston Cup race instead of the deal that was put on."

On Sunday, the race was run as scheduled, with thirteen Cup regulars being joined by drivers from a secondary Grand Touring "pony car" series event that had been run without issues the previous day. Sunday's race was completed without serious incident, although speeds were slower than drivers had run in qualifying. Brickhouse scored his only Cup victory in a Dodge entered by Ray Nichels.

Allison said he listened to the race on radio in his backyard in Hueytown, Alabama. "I had a long, agonizing day," he said. "I didn't want to do anything else—eat, drink, or didn't even want to feel merry."

A BUMPY WORLD 600

That race and its zany circumstances brought back memories of a debut superspeedway race in the first year of the decade. After a swath of construction problems that resulted in financial strain, Charlotte Motor Speedway finally opened June 19, 1960, with a rather audacious race—a 600-miler dubbed the World 600.

Final construction on the track was rushed because earlier work had been snarled by the discovery of bedrock granite at the site. The removal of the granite ate up days and dollars.

Almost immediately, the new track presented problems. During practice, pieces of the speedway came up, leaving potholes. Crews hauled in more than 800 tons of new asphalt for repairs, but issues remained on Sunday—race day.

The pounding of fast cars on the surface caused parts of the track to break apart again, and NASCAR allowed teams to put wire screens on the front of their cars to protect the engine compartments and windshields. That helped to a degree, but cars still were sidelined with blown tires and broken axles. "I don't believe anybody can finish this race in a tank," said Fireball Roberts.

The marathon continued. Jack Smith, a veteran of many laps of NASCAR competition, had a very comfortable five-lap lead late in the day, but a piece of the track ripped into his car's fuel tank, forcing a pit stop. His crew was not able to plug the hole (despite trying to do so with a bar of Camay soap), and Smith parked. Joe Lee Johnson inherited the lead and won the race.

David Pearson pits his Holman–Moody Ford Torino during the 1968 Fireball 300 Cup race at Asheville–Weaverville Speedway on May 5. Pearson went on to capture the victory, one of sixteen he recorded in the 1968 season.

PEARSON'S BIG BREAK

A year later, on that same track, David Pearson began his run to greatness. A star on Carolina's short tracks, Pearson had moved into Cup racing in 1960 and ran well enough to be named rookie of the year. But his big break came when team owner Ray Fox Sr. called and offered a ride in the World 600 in 1961.

Pearson surprised the series stars by winning the 600 despite running the final two laps on a flat tire. He was off and out on a victory parade that ultimately would total 105 victories, second in Cup history only to Richard Petty's 200.

The Wood Brothers, a team with which Pearson would star in the 1970s, put its No. 21 cars at the top of the sport in the 1960s. The team started by Virginian Glen Wood and his brothers rode the ingenuity of crew chief/mechanic Leonard Wood to the front of the grid, building one of the sport's most lasting and successful teams while also revolutionizing pit stops with skill and grace.

TOP: **While LeeRoy Yarbrough didn't have the most wins in the 1969 NASCAR Grand National season, he did have some of the most colorful. Driving for Herb Nab in cars prepared by Junior Johnson, he took the checkers seven times that season, including the Daytona 500 and the Firecracker 400 at Daytona; the Rebel 400 and Southern 500 at Darlington; and the World 600 at Charlotte.**

ABOVE LEFT: **Although his life ended in despair and tragedy, perhaps the most satisfying time of LeeRoy Yarbrough's career was when he celebrated his 1969 Daytona 500 win in Victory Lane with all his many well-wishers.**

ABOVE RIGHT: **As its owner and promoter, H. Clay Earles was the foundation of Martinsville Speedway from its inception in 1947—nearly one year before NASCAR was officially formed—until his death on November 16, 1999. Earles was also a staunch ally of "Big Bill" France, which is perhaps one reason the 0.526-mile track is the only one of NASCAR's original tracks still on the Cup Series schedule. Here Earles addresses the crowd during the Cardinal 500 weekend for NASCAR Modified and Sportsman cars in 1969.**

The Woods' team grew from the roots of an ancient American Beech tree in the yard of the brothers' parents. The five Wood boys were raised in a small farmhouse along Highway 8 near Stuart, Virginia, and Glen grew up loving cars. He and his brothers tinkered with a 1938 Ford coupe, testing its speed on nearby backroads. When the engine needed work, they hung a chain over the strongest limb of the beech tree and hoisted the engine. "We didn't have a skyhook or anything," Glen Wood said. "You did what you had to do."

From such humble beginnings, the Wood boys built a racing empire. The small town of Stuart became famous across the motorsports community as the team enjoyed success both in NASCAR and, notably, in the Indianapolis 500. The team's driver list ultimately would include A. J. Foyt, Cale Yarborough, Dan Gurney, Curtis Turner, Pearson, and an honor roll of others, and the wins stacked up over the years.

In the mid-1960s, Bill France began to realize a dream of building an even bigger and grander racetrack than the Daytona International Speedway. He realized that dream in the 2.66-mile Alabama International Motor Speedway, which held its first Cup Series race on September 14, 1969.

Controversy arose before the racing even began at Talladega as many of the veteran drivers in what was then known as the NASCAR Grand National Series did not believe that tire manufacturers Goodyear and Firestone had produced a safe enough tire. This led a group called the Professional Drivers Association (PDA) to petition Bill France to postpone the race, which he flatly refused to do. He relayed that message to the drivers in this meeting.

After being told by Bill France to race or pack up and get out, Professional Drivers Association members met to discuss their options. In this meeting led by Richard Petty, most of the veteran drivers decided to pack up and go home, meaning France had to fill out the starting field for the 1969 Talladega 500 with journeyman drivers and drivers from a preliminary race held the day before.

A shot of the field at the Alabama International Motor Speedway as it comes to take the green flag for the first time in a Cup Series race. A field of thirty-six cars started the 1969 Talladega 500, the forty-fourth race on the NASCAR Grand National Series schedule that season.

Driving a Dodge Daytona owned by Ray Nichels, relatively unknown driver Richard Brickhouse took the checkered flag in the inaugural race at the Alabama International Motor Speedway on September 14, 1969. Second-place finisher Jim Vandiver led 102 of 188 laps that day, however, and long contended that a scoring error kept him from being the first-ever Talladega Cup Series winner.

Bill France (left) congratulates 1969 Talladega 500 winner Richard Brickhouse at the end of a long, hot race. The race brought an end to a tumultuous weekend in the Alabama countryside for Brickhouse, one of the few veteran drivers who decided to stay and run the race after others boycotted. It was the only win of Brickhouse's Cup Series career.

WINGED CARS TAKE FLIGHT

Near the end of the decade, car manufacturers battled for supremacy on NASCAR's high banks with some of the most striking vehicles in racing history. They were known as winged cars because, in fact, they had wings. The rear-deck pieces rose high above the cars' rear decks and made the cars look like spaceships.

Chrysler led the way in winged-car development. Dodge trimmed the nose on its Charger and then added the rear wing and labeled the car the Dodge Daytona. Its sister Plymouth model was the Superbird.

Richard Brickhouse won in a Dodge Daytona in the boycott-plagued inaugural race at Alabama International Motor Speedway in September 1969, and Pete Hamilton put a Superbird in the victory lane in the 1970 Daytona 500. Ultimately, the cars were too fast, and NASCAR legislated them out of existence.

The turbulent Sixties were at an end.

DAVID PEARSON
(1966, 1968, 1969)

RICHARD PETTY
(1964, 1967)

CHAMPS

Pearson teamed with fellow Spartanburg, South Carolina, resident and car owner Cotton Owens to outrun rookie James Hylton, another upstate South Carolina driver, to win the 1966 championship. Pearson moved to Holman-Moody's solid Ford team and won the 1968 title over his close friend Bobby Isaac. Pearson and Holman-Moody repeated in 1969 as he won 11 of 51 starts. For the rest of his career, Pearson chose to run mainly big-track, big-money races and never pursued the championship again. He closed his career with 105 Cup victories, second only to Richard Petty.

The man who ultimately would hold seven Cup championship trophies won his first in 1964. Petty had won 14 times in 1963 but lost the title to Joe Weatherly. Petty made a stunning 61 starts in 1964, winning his first Daytona 500 and cruising to the championship by more than 5,000 points over Ned Jarrett. He sealed his title of "King" Richard three years later with a sensational season, winning 27 of 48 races, including ten in a row, setting two records that probably will never be challenged. The decade of the sixties built the Petty legend as he became the driver to beat at virtually every stop.

NED JARRETT

(1961, 1965)

JOE WEATHERLY

(1962, 1963)

REX WHITE

(1960)

Jarrett was a big winner in NASCAR's Sportsman series in the 1950s. Having nothing else to prove there, he made numerous attempts to move into the Cup Series in good equipment. Turned back at every corner, he eventually bought a top-flight car during the 1959 season, paying for it with a check that he covered only by winning his first two Cup races that weekend. From there, Jarrett was a consistent winner at NASCAR's top level, totaling 50 victories and a pair of championships before retiring after the 1966 season. His standout victory came in the 1965 Southern 500, which he won by 14 laps over Buck Baker.

Weatherly was an American Motorcyclist Association champion and wasted no time transferring that talent to four wheels when he moved into NASCAR. In 1962, his first full season in the Cup Series, he teamed up with car owner Bud Moore to win the championship. Moore decided to run fewer races in 1963, so Weatherly put together a laundry list of other owners to run enough races to score a second straight championship. Sadly, Weatherly was killed early the next season in a crash on the Riverside, California, road course.

White's career at the top level of NASCAR was short but productive. After success in short-track Sportsman racing, he built a Cup team in Spartanburg, South Carolina, and, with the help of crew chief/mechanic Louis Clements, put together six wins and a string of consistently strong finishes to win the championship. His average finish across 40 starts was 5.3. White totaled 28 victories in a Cup career that lasted only from 1956 to 1964.

Many drivers of his era believed that no matter what type of car or series A. J. Foyt was running, he was one of the best racers ever to strap on a helmet. Here Foyt (50) races Richard Petty (43) during the 1973 Daytona 500 race at Daytona International Speedway. Petty scored the victory that day while Foyt finished fourth, but Foyt had won the previous year in the 1972 Daytona 500 by lapping the entire field.

Chapter 3

THE 1970s

Shifting into High Gear

By Al Pearce

IT CAN BE ARGUED with certainty that NASCAR grew more in the 1970s than at any era in its seventy-five-year history. The entire face of what had been a fairly small, modest, regional sports enterprise run by one man exploded almost overnight into a national motorsports franchise that touched almost every corner of the country.

As unlikely as it seems, much of that growth can be traced to controversial federal legislation that worked its way through the Congress of the United States from the late sixties into the early seventies.

For the first time, major sponsorships emerged in every nook and cranny of NASCAR. The schedule changed dramatically, trimmed from upward of fifty events in the late sixties to a more reasonable thirty-some in the seventies. Many of the sport's traditional short tracks disappeared from the shortened schedule. Dirt tracks—the venue of choice for almost twenty years—were gone by 1973.

Most of these dramatic changes were fueled by an injection of money into the sport. In the early seventies, NASCAR signed on with a major corporation willing to spend its own money to promote and underwrite major-league racing. That opportunity came thanks to new laws banning the advertisement of tobacco products from radio and television.

With untold millions of advertising dollars suddenly available, NASCAR and its leadership found itself as comfortable on Wall Street in New York as it had always been on International Speedway Boulevard in Daytona Beach.

CHANGING THE FACE OF STOCK CAR RACING

On April 1, 1970, after several years of negotiation, President Richard Nixon signed the Public Health Cigarette Smoking Act. First introduced in 1969, the bill finally passed the House and Senate, then went to the Oval Office for the president's signature. Nixon, who favored pipes over cigarettes or cigars, enacted the new law at the urging of public health officials. Almost all

Driving the famous Holman-Moody No. 17 Ford, David Pearson is on his way to a second-place finish in the February 22 running of the 1970 Daytona 500 at Daytona International Speedway.

NASCAR President Bill France Sr. congratulates Buddy Baker after he became the first NASCAR driver to break the 200-mph mark on a closed circuit on Tuesday, March 24, 1970. Driving this Dodge Daytona during a tire test at the Alabama International Motor Speedway, Baker reached a speed of 200.477 mph on the 2.66-mile track.

of them—even those who posed for smoking ads in newspapers and magazines—cited numerous studies tying tobacco use to health issues, specifically cancer and heart attacks. The legislation, passed after more than a year of debate, went into effect on New Year's Day 1971. (The last televised cigarette commercial ran during *The Johnny Carson Show* late that night). The new law left tobacco companies with millions of available dollars from their radio/TV budgets.

In the 1970 season, NASCAR allowed "winged" cars to race, and they so dominated the circuit that Dodge Daytonas and Plymouth Superbirds were quickly outlawed by the sanctioning body. Here Bobby Isaac (71) and Bobby Allison (22), driving Dodge Charger Daytonas, battle three-wide with the Ford Torino Talladega of James Hylton (No. 48) during a 1970 Cup Series race.

The No. 71 Dodge Daytona owned by Nord Krauskopf, sponsored by K&K Insurance, and driven by Bobby Isaac was one of the most legendary of all the winged cars run on the NASCAR Grand National circuit in 1970. When NASCAR banned the winged cars prior to the 1971 season, Isaac took it to the Bonneville Salt Flats and, over the course of a few days, set twenty-eight land speed records over various categories.

Richard Petty (43) leads James Hylton (No. 48) and Pete Hamilton (6) during the Valentine's Day 1971 Daytona 500. The previous season, Hamilton had driven a Plymouth Superbird winged car for Petty Enterprises, winning the Daytona 500 as well as the Alabama 500 and Talladega 500 at the Alabama International Motor Speedway.

The oft-told story says former bootlegger-turned-driver-turned-owner Robert Glenn "Junior" Johnson approached a friend who worked for R. J. Reynolds Tobacco Co. in nearby Winston-Salem, North Carolina. He asked the man, an RJR sales manager, whether the company might want to sponsor the No. 98 Ford Torino that Johnson planned to campaign in 1971 for LeeRoy Yarbrough. The friend brokered a meeting between Johnson and two ranking RJR executives. When Johnson suggested an annual sponsorship of $800,000, the executives almost laughed in his face.

They said they had plenty of money—several accounts have mentioned $570,000,000—at their disposal. Stunned, Johnson promptly called NASCAR founder/president Bill France with the news that they easily had enough to sponsor the entire series, known then as Grand National. It wasn't long before France dispatched trusted aides Jim Foster and Roger Bear to Winston-Salem to meet with RJR shortly before Christmas of 1970.

"We had come up with three parts to the sponsorship proposal for Reynolds," said Bear, now retired after several decades as a prominent motorsports executive. "One was a $100,000 point fund to encourage more teams to run the full schedule. Another was changing the name of the Alabama 500 at Talladega to the Winston 500. And we changed the January race at Riverside, California, from the Riverside 500 to the Winston West 500. Later, we added sponsorship of NASCAR's entire West Coast tour and called it the Winston West Series. It was only a few days after the meeting in North Carolina that people at Reynolds got back to us and said yes."

After the R. J. Reynolds Tobacco Company became the Cup Series title sponsor in 1971, the Winston name became synonymous with NASCAR racing at all levels. R. J. Reynolds left the sport in 2003.

The historic announcement was delivered in January 1971. It addressed the unprecedented $100,000 point fund to be paid out after one-third, two-thirds, and the end of the season. With the 1971 schedule already in place, teams faced only one more long schedule of forty-eight races. Beginning in 1972 and extending through the rest of the decade, teams would race twenty-eight to thirty-one times annually. Only much later did the schedule reach the current thirty-six events.

So it was that RJR and NASCAR began their business relationship that lasted from 1971 until 2003, when Congress got even more restrictive about tobacco advertising. Beginning in the "glory days" of 1971, the new sponsor plastered images of its red-and-white flagship Winston cigarette brand almost everywhere. It poured money into point funds, race purses, and special awards for on-track performances. It ensured that almost everyone walking onto a NASCAR speedway—regardless of size, location, or the program—knew they were guests of one of America's largest cigarette manufacturers.

By 1972's season-opening Daytona 500, the long-familiar Grand National Series had been renamed the Winston Cup Grand National Series. (It was quickly shortened to simply Winston Cup). RJR's innovative new Sports Marketing Enterprise spent an estimated $15 million (in the early years) to $40 million (toward the end) to advertise its products. In addition to stock cars, the

GUARDIAN OF VICTORY LANE

The name Bill Brodrick likely didn't ring familiar with many NASCAR fans throughout the 1970s. But the image of a muscular 6-foot-3 man with long, flaming-red hair, a "Grizzly Adams" beard, and designer shades in Victory Lane…now *that* man was as familiar as a checkered flag.

For 29 years—beginning in 1969 and going through the 70s, '80s, and late into the '90s—Brodrick had more victory moments than anybody in racing. He was the unmistakable "Hat Man" who deftly handled all the marketing and PR needs of winning drivers, their owners, and sponsors, plus television partners, NASCAR officials, media photographers and writers, and family members.

The Cincinnati native, now 83, ran Victory Lane with a velvet hammer. He decided who got in and, more importantly, who wasn't needed at that moment. He directed the parade of corporate well-wishers and ensured the race's celebrities got their share of attention. He told photographers and cameramen where to set up and when they were cleared to shoot. Few people had his patience for turning what might have become chaos into a professional, smooth-running, joyous celebration.

But his most famous skill set was managing to get the winning driver and everyone on his team to constantly change freshly distributed hats so photographers could snap photos for various sponsors. In time, almost certainly because of his compelling appearance, he became a racing institution. He signed autographs, had his own trading card, registered "The Hat Man" trademark, and was a quickly recognized in public as any driver in the world.

He worked in the PR and marketing division of Union Oil Co. from 1969 until Tosco bought the company in 1997. Without explanation and out of the blue, Tosco dismissed him after NASCAR's 1997 season finale. He retired to the Chicago suburb of Algonquin to run a tavern near the Fox River. If he has regrets, he doesn't publicly express them.

"The power of television made me who I became," he said a few years ago. "The nature of what I did got me known. And the fans … the best in the world never forgot me and were always happy to see me. They made it all happen for me. I was the luckiest guy in the world because I looked forward to it every day for 29 years. I wish it had been 30 years so I could have had sort of a one-year farewell tour."

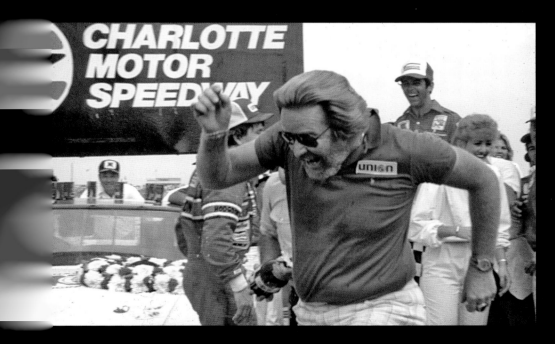

Bill Brodrick was a fixture in NASCAR victory lanes for many years as the official representative of Union 76.

FROM "STOCK" TO HANDBUILT

Except for maybe the very first race or two, there's never been anything exactly "stock" about "stock cars." NASCAR meant well when it included the word "stock" in its corporate name, but "sorta-stock" might have been more appropriate. In fact, the first eight-race season of 1949 of what eventually became today's Cup Series was called "Strictly Stock."

During the 1950s and increasingly in the 1960s, a few safety-related modifications were the only things separating "Strictly Stock" race cars from street-legal showroom cars. Teams were allowed to beef up brakes, remove items associated with passenger comfort, install safety belts, tape over headlights, and chain shut the doors. Drivers often drove their street cars to the track, raced them, then drove them back home. Hall of Fame driver Hershel McGriff of Oregon did that to run the first Southern 500 in 1950.

Things changed dramatically in the 1960s and early 1970s as "stock cars" evolved into purpose-built race cars. Ex-racer Banjo Matthews led the way after leaving the cockpit in 1963 to work for Ford Racing through its deal with Holman-Moody Racing. "Banjo hand-built the body and framework and Holman-Moody put in the motors," said NASCAR historian Buzz McKim. "After Ford left racing, Banjo opened his own shop in 1970 and built cars for Chevrolet, and later for others. On many occasions, cars built by Banjo comprised over half the field. He quickly became the best in the business."

Banjo's Performance Center in western North Carolina was revered for producing amazingly competitive cars. He used a chassis jig and surface plate bought from Ralph Moody to bend and shape and mold with loving detail the chassis and rollbars of what became Grand National cars. His contributions extended not only to on-track performance, but to safety issues as well. It has been documented that nobody ever died racing a Banjo-built car.

According to McKim in *Street Muscle* magazine, his individually produced chassis—the manufacturer's engine and sheet metal didn't seem to matter—won 262 of 362 Cup Series races from 1974–1985. Included in those numbers were all 30 races in 1978 (ten of them by Cale Yarborough) and consecutive championships in 1975, 1976, 1977, and 1978 from Richard Petty and Yarborough. Other builders began following Matthews' chassis guidelines, but nobody else seemed to get it exactly right.

"The basic construction of a car is not what wins races," he once said. "It's the team effort after the car leaves our facility that separates the winners and losers. We strive to build our cars as good for one customer as we do for another. The credit for their performance goes to the people who operate them."

Legendary owner/builder Smokey said this about his friendly rival, who died in 1996: "When we go back and look at what he did for racers, fans, and the industry, Banjo Matthews was probably one of the twenty-five main building blocks of stock car racing."

After retiring as a driver, Banjo Matthews took on the role of car owner and builder. Matthews is shown here working on his 1964 Ford. Junior Johnson was the driver.

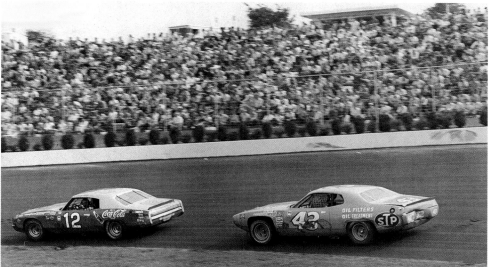

ABOVE LEFT: **Appropriately attired in her Winston outfit and matching hat, Miss Winston poses for a photo with David Pearson, in Victory Lane after Pearson won one of his three Winston 500 Cup Series races at Alabama International Motor Speedway in the early 1970s.**

ABOVE RIGHT: **Bill France Sr. shares a moment with his son Bill France Jr. in 1972. "Big Bill" retired on January 10, 1972, and "Little Bill" became NASCAR's chief executive officer. He served in that capacity until 2000.**

Bobby Allison (12) leads Richard Petty (43) during a 1972 Cup Series race. To the delight of NASCAR fans everywhere, the pair had an ongoing feud during that season, which ended with Petty winning eight races and his sixth career Cup Series championship. Though Allison won ten races, he lost the championship to Petty by 128 points.

In one of the most unlikely victories in Cup Series history, Dick Brooks, shown here battling Bobby Allison (12), won the 1973 Talladega 500 run on August 12. Brooks picked up the ride in the Crawford Brothers No. 22 Plymouth just three days before the race and went on to score the upset victory—the only victory of his Cup Series career.

company also supported drag racing with the National Hot Rod Association, sports car racing with the International Motor Sports Association, and hydroplanes with the American Power Boat Association.

There was motorcycle racing with the American Motorcyclist Association, a coast-to-coast professional rodeo series, and professional golf and tennis tours. There was hardly a professional sport in America that RJR and its brands did not touch.

It's difficult to estimate the company's financial commitment to racing during those thirty-three years. There eventually came an annual postseason champion's payoff of at least $1 million. There were additional millions spent to upgrade and modernize speedways themselves. Corporate VIP suites appeared at every track. There were improvements to red-and-white scoreboards. Outdated press boxes and media centers were refurbished to handle the expanding media outlets. Several former RJR executives have said the bottom line might have been $50 million a year. Apparently, the NASCAR portion of RJR's budget had no ceiling.

The late Paul Sawyer and his sons, Billy and the late Wayne Sawyer, owned and ran the 0.5-mile Richmond Fairgrounds Raceway in 1971. The new sponsorship agreement allowed smaller tracks like Richmond, Martinsville, and North Wilkesboro to spend advertising money it didn't have. In almost every case, RJR freely spent more money on NASCAR's member tracks than they could possibly have spent themselves.

"People from RJR came into Richmond two or three weeks before our races and painted everything red and white," Billy Sawyer recently recalled. "They put up posters and banners advertising the race. You know, name of the event, when and what time, what day. Big, colorful posters in stores and buildings. They'd advertise NASCAR on radio and TV, on billboards, in grocery stores, and gas stations. They had a fleet of show cars they drove all over town. They gave free tickets to their commercial clients. And there's no way to gauge the importance of RJR and NASCAR taking its Cup Series awards banquet to New York (in December of 1981). Being at the Waldorf Astoria was a big, big deal for stock car racing."

Almost overnight throughout the 1970s, RJR splashed its paint all over every NASCAR track. "Ralph Seagraves (head of RJR's new Sports Marketing Division) wanted nice tracks," Bear said. "Paint didn't cost much, so Ralph had his people go everywhere and paint everything. Not just the big tracks that got the Sunday races, but the short, weekly tracks that were part of the (lower level) Winston Racing Series. Officials wore red-and-white outfits. Track signage was all red and white. Drivers had Winston patches on their uniforms and wore Winston caps. There was no mistaking who was sponsoring the races. It was a great time to be working in NASCAR."

Just when it looked like Benny Parsons' championship dream had gone up in smoke following a terrible wreck on lap thirteen of the October 21, 1973 American 500 at North Carolina Motor Speedway, a NASCAR miracle of sorts took place. Crew members from other teams came over to help—some even taking parts from their own cars—and after just over an hour, they had Parsons back in the race. Thanks to all the help, Parsons finished the season finale 184 laps behind winner Cale Yarborough, but still claimed the only title of his twenty-one-year Cup Series career by sixty-seven points.

Before becoming president and general manager of Charlotte Motor Speedway in 1975, H. A. "Humpy" Wheeler (right) was director of racing for Firestone Tire & Rubber Company. Here he talks tires with "Crash" Grant of rival Goodyear at a NASCAR Cup Series race.

RIGHT: **Driving a limited schedule in the famed Wood Brothers No. 21 Purolator Ford from 1972 through early 1979, David Pearson won an incredible 43 races in just 143 Cup Series starts. Shown here in a 1974 race, Pearson won seven races in his nineteen starts during that season.**

Jim Vandiver (31) leads Benny Parsons (72) during the Firecracker 400 Cup Series race at Daytona International Speedway on July 4, 1974. At that time, the Firecracker 400 was held on the Fourth of July, regardless of which day of the week the holiday happened to fall on. The race always started at 10 a.m. Eastern time so families could come see the race and still have plenty of time to hit Daytona's beautiful sandy beaches.

Driving Roger Penske's AMC Matador, Bobby Allison (16) leads Cale Yarborough (11) and Richard Petty (43) during the running of the Virginia 500 Cup Series race at Martinsville Speedway on April 27, 1975. Allison finished fourth that day, but by season's end, he had put the Matador in Victory Lane for Penske three times.

A MONUMENTAL CHANGE

If the arrival of RJR was the biggest off-track story of the 1970s, the change at the head of NASCAR's boardroom table was tied for No. 1. For the first time since the organization's founding in the late 1940s, William Henry Getty France was no longer (publicly) in charge.

"Bill Big" became head of American stock car racing when he summoned like-minded men to Daytona Beach's oceanfront Streamline Hotel in December of 1947. The former driver, mechanic, promoter, official, and businessman aimed to bring national order to the new type of racing that featured showroom-legal family cars. Despite starting out with two dozen associates, there was no doubt after the three-day meeting who would be in charge.

France was a huge (6-foot-6) man with great charisma. He stood down to no man and commanded every scene, as much by his stature as by his "persuasive" nature of getting his point across. Those others at the Streamline during those formative days knew better than to cross him. (Later, in the 1950s and 1960s, some of racing's biggest stars learned just how stubborn and vindictive he could be).

Oh, he accepted advice and listened to suggestions from others—he was smart enough to realize he didn't know everything—but make no mistake: NASCAR was his baby and his *way* was the *only* way. His rules were generally iron fisted. If you didn't like them, he'd show you the door). But to France's everlasting credit, while perhaps a half-dozen other sanctioning bodies wanted to rule the sport, "Big Bill" had the uncanny knack of looking ahead, seeing what had to be done, and convincing naysayers that his way was the best.

And thus, he ruled from day one until retiring on January 10, 1972. He had brought stock car racing to the point where rules were (generally) uniformly enforced at NASCAR-sanctioned tracks. Being a NASCAR member meant accepting the organization's technical, administrative, and competition rules or moving on. Under his semidictatorial leadership and with RJR's help, NASCAR expanded from a few Modified and Strictly Stock races primarily in the East and Northeast to upwards of fifty races at speedways from coast to coast.

He stayed in control until he handed the keys to his firstborn, William Clifton France. (He technically wasn't a junior, but quickly became known as "Bill Jr.") The son held a tight rein on what his father had created, watching over racing and making business decisions from his modest office at Daytona International Speedway. He ran the show until 2003, when he retired at sixty-seven and gave control of the organization to his son, Brian Zachary France.

Brian ran things until 2018, when embarrassing public missteps in the New York City area brought about his dismissal from the management team. His uncle, Jim France, briefly led NASCAR before giving way to current president Steve Phelps. Several other men briefly occupied the leadership role—whether called president, CEO, COO, or Chairman—including Mike Helton, Brent Dewar, and Steve O'Donnell, until Phelps assumed command in 2018.

Seeing Richard Petty surrounded by media members and well-wishers in Victory Lane was a common occurrence throughout the 1970s. Here he visits Victory Lane with his STP Dodge after winning the 1975 Firecracker 400 Cup Series race at Daytona International Speedway.

TOP LEFT: **Coming out of Turn 4 and heading for home on the final lap of the 1976 Daytona 500, it looked like Richard Petty would win the sixth Great American Race of his career, but it was not to be. David Pearson, who had dogged Petty all day in the No. 21 Wood Brothers Mercury, approached Petty as they entered the Daytona International Speedway tri-oval area, causing both drivers to crash into the concrete retaining wall.**

TOP RIGHT: **After spinning into the grass following his crash with David Pearson on the last lap of the 1976 Daytona 500, Richard Petty tries desperately to restart his No. 43 STP Dodge while Pearson (21) slowly inches his way toward the Daytona International Speedway finish line. Pearson was able to keep his car in gear and make it to the finish line to score the victory.**

ABOVE LEFT: **In Victory Lane, David Pearson tries to explain one of the most incredible finishes in Cup Series history. Despite suffering tremendous damage in a last-lap crash with Richard Petty in the 1976 Daytona 500, Pearson was able to win his third Great American Race by driving across the finish line using the engine's starter motor.**

GETTING SMALLER TO BECOME BIGGER

When R. J. Reynolds arrived in 1971, it asked NASCAR to significantly reduce the Grand National schedule to a manageable number of events. With almost no argument, NASCAR did exactly that.

Throughout the 1960s and into the early 1970s, teams often ran upwards of sixty-plus races a year. It often seemed they barely arrived home from one race before leaving for another. Teams chasing the championship and its modest season-ending payoffs often raced three times a week: short-track events on Wednesday and Friday nights, followed by a superspeedway race on Sunday afternoon. The heaviest pre-RJR schedule in the sport's first twenty years was sixty-two races in 1964. (Ned Jarrett won fifteen of his fifty-nine starts that year, but Richard Petty won the championship with a nine-for-sixty-one effort).

ABOVE LEFT: **Cale Yarborough celebrated our nation's bicentennial by winning the Firecracker 400 at Daytona International Speedway on July 4, 1976. It was Yarborough's fourth win of the season, and he went on to finish with nine. Yarborough won the Cup Series championship that year, the first of three consecutive championship wins for the Timmonsville, South Carolina, driver.**

ABOVE RIGHT: **During their long Cup Series careers, David Pearson and Cale Yarborough traded sheet metal many times. Here Pearson (21) tries to hold off Yarborough (11) in a 1976 race at Martinsville Speedway.**

After forty-eight races each in 1970 and 1971, teams were delighted to see a trimmed-down thirty-one-race schedule in 1972, the first year of the "modern era." Gone were the frequent midweek races at such bullrings as Hampton and South Boston in Virginia; Hickory, Asheville, and Winston-Salem in North Carolina; Columbia and Greenville in South Carolina; and Augusta, Savannah, and Macon in Georgia. Also gone were the northeastern tracks at Trenton, Islip, Malta, Thompson, Bridgehampton, and Oxford. The rationale behind the change was that fewer races with larger purses in larger markets intensified the importance of each race. And in time, RJR executives acknowledged the difficulty in properly servicing two or three races a week.

NASCAR and RJR recognized the hardship on short tracks when they lost their Grand National dates. For many tracks, not having Petty, Allison, Pearson, and others once or twice a year was a devastating loss. In response, RJR poured millions into its new weekly Winston Racing Series, helping weekly tracks upgrade their facilities, improve their purses, and help crown regional and national champions.

HELLO TO NEW TRACKS, SO LONG TO OTHERS

As RJR spent millions promoting and advertising the rebranded Winston Cup Series, a handful of new venues emerged. The one-mile Dover Downs Speedway in Delaware, the massive 2.66-mile Talladega Superspeedway in Alabama, the two-mile Michigan Speedway near Detroit, and the three-sided, 2.5-mile Pocono Raceway in rural Pennsylvania opened to enthusiastic race fans. Those tracks established themselves in the early 1970s and remain on the Cup Series schedule to this day.

But there were failures too. The two-mile Texas World Speedway at College Station and the 2.5-mile Ontario Motor Speedway in southern California hosted thirteen races throughout the 1970s before going away. TWS hosted eight of them—one in 1969, five in the 1970s, and two in the early 1980s—before leaving NASCAR in 1981. Located in the rural scrubland of southcentral Texas, it never quite caught on with fans in that part of the country.

In contrast, OMS was deemed far more valuable as a commercial real estate tract near Los Angeles. It hosted eight races in the 1970s and one in 1980 before developers bought the land, razed the speedway, and built yet another shopping mall. Ironically, Benny Parsons, who had won the last Cup Series race at South Boston (Virginia) Speedway in 1971, also won the last Cup races at College Station and Ontario.

In its early years NASCAR was primarily a dirt-based series. Except for that paved portion of Highway A1A along the 4.10-mile highway/beach course in Daytona Beach, nineteen of the first twenty-one Cup Series races were wholly or partially on dirt. The first all-paved venue was the 1.25-mile (later extended to 1.37 miles) Darlington Raceway in northeastern South Carolina. The legendary "Lady In Black" or "Track Too Tough to Tame" hosted its first 500-mile Southern 500 Classic on Labor Day of 1950. Seventy-five cars qualified and spent more than 6½ hours circling the jam-packed speedway 400 times before Johnny Mantz finally beat Fireball Roberts by nine laps.

Pavement gradually replaced dirt, but NASCAR doggedly clung to its roots by running a few dirt-track races deep into 1971. Perhaps appropriately, Richard Petty won the last dirt-track race, a 100-lap, 100-mile event at Raleigh, North Carolina, in September of that year. Stock car purists don't consider the recent dirt-over-pavement races at 0.5-mile Bristol, Tennessee, as "real" dirt-track races.

Richard Petty (43) and Darrell Waltrip (88) race side by side as Benny Parsons (72) closes in during a 1977 Cup Series race at Riverside International Raceway. From 1958 to 1988, Riverside hosted forty-eight Cup Series events, and in 1965 and in every season from 1970 to 1981, the Cup Series season opener was run on the 2.62-mile road course.

CREAM RISES TO THE TOP

One of racing's oldest and most-quoted adages goes like this: money buys speed; how fast do you want to go?

As always in motorsports, a handful of high-profile teams and drivers with solid financial resources dominated the entire decade of the 1970s. Except for an occasional upset—but certainly infrequently—six future Hall of Fame drivers won almost 79 percent of the 336 races between 1970 and 1979. Richard Petty (eighty-nine victories), Cale Yarborough (fifty-two), David Pearson (forty-seven), Bobby Allison (forty), relative newcomer Darrell Waltrip (twenty-two), and Bobby Isaac (sixteen) combined for 266 victories. (Hall of Fame drivers Buddy Baker and Benny Parsons—each with fourteen victories—were the decade's only other double-figure winners).

In addition, Petty won five of the decade's ten Winston Cup championship trophies and was points runner-up twice. Yarborough won three consecutive titles and also was runner-up twice. Parsons and Isaac each won one championship. Allison finished second in points three times, and Waltrip, Dave Marcis, and James Hylton each finished second once. While the on-track competition was acceptable, it always seemed the same half-dozen drivers were winning most of the time.

The cost of winning has always been high, as much so in the 1970s as at any other time. Ambitious ownership groups like Petty Enterprises, Junior Johnson and Associates, DiGard Racing, Wood Brothers Racing, and Holman-Moody spared no expense. Relatively conservative owners Nord Krauskopf and L. G. DeWitt managed to break the big teams' dominance, each winning one of the decade's two remaining championships.

The Cup Series garage could sometimes be a lonely place for Janet Guthrie as she broke NASCAR's gender barrier in the late 1970s. Driving the No. 68 Lynda Ferreri Kelly Girl Chevrolet on the Winston Cup circuit from 1976 to 1978, Guthrie competed in a total of thirty-one races and recorded five top-ten finishes. Her best overall showing came in the 1977 Volunteer at Bristol International Speedway, where she started ninth and came home sixth.

Dale Earnhardt competes in the eighth Cup Series race of his career, driving the No. 96 Cardinal Tractor Ford owned by Will Cronkite in the 1978 Talladega 500 on August 6. Earnhardt started twenty-seventh on that day and finished twelfth, one spot ahead of Bill Elliott, who was driving the No. 9 Dahlonega Ford Sales Mercury owned by his father George, in his twenty-fifth cup series.

TV FINALLY DISCOVERS NASCAR

Network television had almost ignored stock car racing throughout its early years. In time, though, ABC's popular *Wide World of Sports* anthology series discovered the sport...but only on a limited basis. Although some of its segments were televised live on Saturday afternoon, *WWOS* occasionally slipped in clips of the previous weekend's NASCAR race. It fell far short of what would come later, but at least it was a start and NASCAR was delighted to get it.

Two televised races awakened the rest of America to what the Southeast had known for two decades.

In February of 1976, superstars Pearson and Petty crashed into each other in the final turn on the final lap of the Daytona 500. Petty had led the previous eleven laps when he took the white "one to go" flag just ahead of Pearson, his respected but fiercest rival. They banged together when Pearson tried to pass in Turn 4 coming for the checkered. After fighting for control, both slammed into the outside wall.

In the first NASCAR Cup Series race ever broadcast live, flag-to-flag and coast-to-coast, CBS television viewers were treated to a racing war between Cale Yarborough (11) and Donnie Allison (No. 1) over the final few laps of the 1979 Daytona 500. On the final lap, the two would crash each other out going into Turn 3 and, as they say, all hell broke loose.

RIGHT: **As the discussion about the ending of the 1979 Daytona 500 between Donnie Allison and Cale Yarborough continued to heat up with CBS national television viewers looking on, Donnie's brother, Bobby Allison, drove up and stopped in Turn 3 to ask Donnie if he needed a ride. At that point, Yarborough began "discussing" things with Bobby Allison as well, eventually shoving his helmet in the driver's side window and cutting Bobby Allison on the bridge of his nose.**

The fight is on between Cale Yarborough and Bobby Allison following the controversial conclusion of the 1979 Daytona 500. Yarborough, in white, tries to hit Allison with his helmet as Allison tries to grab Yarborough's ankle to bring him to the ground.

Once Bobby Allison was able to regain his footing, he landed several blows, or, as he is fond of saying, "Cale began to beat on my fist with his nose." The skirmishes were soon broken up, and the cross words were eventually forgotten, but the race continues to be one of the most remembered in NASCAR history.

Richard Petty certainly must have liked the 0.5-mile track known as Dover Downs International Speedway in Dover, Delaware, because he won seven races there in his career. Here he takes the checkered flag on September 16 in the 1979 CRC Chemicals 500 by a half-car length over Donnie Allison.

The sight of Richard Petty being presented a trophy in Victory Lane was commonplace in the 1970s as he won 89 of the 336 Cup Series races run in the decade. That means Petty won just over one quarter of all the Cup Series races contested in the 1970s. Here he admires the Governor's Cup trophy after winning the 1979 Daytona 500, breaking a forty-five-race streak of no victories.

Pearson managed to keep his No. 21 Mercury running and limped slowly toward the flagstand. Petty, whose No. 43 Dodge wouldn't refire, bump-started his car for several hundred yards to finish second. That portion of the race was live—the earlier laps were not—and footage of the spectacular finish quickly emerged on every news and sports program that night. Perhaps surprisingly, neither driver held any serious grudge toward the other. NASCAR couldn't have been happier with the outcome, regardless of the winner.

Three years later, fate smiled on Petty on the last lap of the 1979 Daytona 500. He was running a distant third in the season opener when leader Donnie Allison and second-running Cale Yarborough wrecked each other against the outside wall on the backstretch. As they slid together down the Turn 3 banking and onto the apron, a gleefully surprised Petty flashed by en route to the sixth of his seven Daytona 500 victories.

That 500 was the first "Great American Race" televised live from start to finish on network (CBS) television. A massive blizzard had shut down most sports east of the Mississippi that weekend, leaving millions of Americans with nothing to watch on Sunday afternoon TV except the NASCAR race. The spectacular finish—and the postrace fight among Yarborough and the Allison brothers at the accident scene—took the country by storm.

Indeed, it's generally accepted by NASCAR historians that the 1979 Daytona 500 was the most important race in stock car history. (Others say the inaugural 1993 Brickyard 400 was bigger; the argument likely will rage on forever). Combined, that 1979 race's unexpected finish, the postrace fight, Petty's last-lap victory ahead of Waltrip and A. J. Foyt, and the presence of live network TV from start to finish led to the inevitable "water-cooler talk" that dominated the following week in every corner of America.

In many places, the final minute of the 500 and the fight were headlined on the Sunday night news and front-page news the next morning.

SERIES GETS A "WATER-COOLER" RACE

By the middle of the 1970s, NASCAR's premier Cup Series was beginning to slowly gain some traction in America's sports consciousness. As a start, stock car racing had become hugely popular in the Southeast and along the Eastern seaboard. Major races often attracted upwards of 100,000 fans and regional media. And television had finally discovered what Southerners had been bragging about for years. Compared to previous decades, the sport was doing well.

But nationally, racing still lagged behind college basketball and football, professional football and baseball, and the occasional major golf and tennis tournaments. The media generally tolerated racing, but displayed no deep-seated interest in closely following it. Even with popular superstar Richard Petty leading the way, many of America's sports fans still looked down on racing.

One race midway through the '70s helped NASCAR begin to change that perception.

The 1976 Daytona 500 is generally considered to have produced either the greatest finish in stock car history or the second-greatest. (Certainly, the 1979 Daytona 500 is in the conversation). The '76 season-opener was on Sunday afternoon, February 15 at Daytona International Speedway. It involved two of the sport's all-time best drivers in the year's most important race.

Mercury-driving David Pearson and Dodge-driving Petty began the last lap of the annual event locked together, Petty leading by several car-length. Pearson, famous for being crafty and opportunistic, was content to stay second until dipping low to pass entering Turn 3. He went by cleanly and easily moved up in front of Petty. A second later, in Turn 4, Petty countered with a low-side pass of his own to briefly regain the lead.

But Petty misjudged the gap as he moved over to clear Pearson along the short chute. They touched off Turn 4, lost control, slammed the outside wall, and began sliding toward the start/finish line, about 600 yards distant. Despite heavy damage, Pearson kept keep his car running; Petty's heavily damaged car stalled in the tri-oval grass and wouldn't restart. He could do nothing but watch in frustration as Pearson chugged past, taking the checkered flag at perhaps 25 miles per hour.

"Nobody knew it then, but that was the race that got everything going," long-time motorsports writer and broadcaster Dr. Dick Berggren said years later. "It was the first 'water cooler' race, the first time that people had stood around water coolers on Monday and talked about seeing a race on TV the day before. It took a while—years, maybe—to realize how important it was."

The field gets set for a restart after a caution flag during the 1976 Daytona 500. Leader David Pearson (21) lines up on the outside of row one with Frank Warren (79) on the inside. Pearson went on to win the race in a thrilling, crashing finish with Richard Petty.

Former Cup Series driving champion turned broadcaster Ned Jarrett (left) interviews Dale Earnhardt during a Motor Racing Network broadcast of a race during the 1979 season. Earnhardt burst onto the NASCAR scene in a big way that season, winning a race, finishing seventh in the Cup Series championship chase, and earning Rookie of the Year honors.

A CHANGE OF THE GUARD

While Richard Petty, the Allison brothers, Cale Yarborough, David Pearson, Buddy Baker, and Bobby Isaac dominated the decade, change was on the way. Waltrip brought his considerable talent, brashness, and arrogance to Cup racing in the early 1970s. No less the authority that long-time Charlotte Motor Speedway promoter H. A. "Humpy" Wheeler once anointed him, "one of the two or three most important drivers the sport has ever had. The entire face of racing changed when he began winning. He made everyone else get better, both on and off the track."

Likewise, the appearance of second-generation driver Dale Earnhardt toward the end of the 1970s would have an enormous impact on the sport for two decades. While Waltrip introduced "flash and dash" sophistication to the sport for the first time, Earnhardt was the rough-and-tumble, take-no-prisoners bully. Beloved in his native central North Carolina, "the Intimidator" appealed more to NASCAR's beer-and-barbecue crowd than Waltrip's wine-and-cheese set back in Nashville.

Future stars Harry Gant, Sterling Marlin, Ricky Rudd, and Neil Bonnett, and champions-in-waiting Benny Parsons and Bill Elliott, also reached the Cup level between 1970 and 1979. Elliott and his family-owned team from Georgia's backwoods attracted fans through their quiet, no-frills, heads-down way of going from being almost unnoticed to superstars. Elliott, his brothers Ernie and Dan, and their father, George, quietly worked their way up the ladder without much hype or hoopla, reaching the Cup Series championship stage in 1988. By the time he retired in 2012, Bill had won forty-four times and been named the most popular driver thirteen times during a sixteen-year run.

The decade produced only twelve first-time winners. With Petty, Pearson, Yarborough, Allison, Isaac, and Waltrip winning almost 79 percent of the events, there were precious few checkered flags available for everyone else. Pete Hamilton and James Hylton broke through in 1970; Ray Elder and Parsons in 1971; Mark Donohue and Dick Brooks in 1973; Earl Ross in 1974; Waltrip and Dave Marcis in 1975; Neil Bonnett in 1977; Lennie Pond in 1978; and Earnhardt in 1979. The victories by Donohue, Brooks, Ross, and Pond were for each of them the only one of their careers.

SPECIAL AWARDS AND REWARDS

Executives at RJR created the Winston All-Star Race that Waltrip won in 1985 at Charlotte Motor Speedway. They also created the Winston Million, a four-race series paying $1 million to anyone who won three of four "Crown Jewel" events: Daytona 500, Winston 500, Coca-Cola 600, and Southern 500. Elliott was the first Winston Million champion by winning the 1985 races at Daytona Beach, Charlotte, and Darlington. RJR spent a small fortune in qualifying awards and in the postseason awards banquet that went to New York City for the first time in 1981.

The 1970s produced a mixed bag of Rookie of the Year winners. Rudd and Earnhardt went on to great success. By comparison, neither Bill Dennis, Walter Ballard, Larry Smith, Skip Manning, Ronnie Thomas, nor Bruce Hill ever won. Lennie Pond and Earl Ross each won once in their short-lived careers.

Another of NASCAR's all-time most iconic paint schemes is the Busch Beer scheme on this Junior Johnson Oldsmobile driven by Cale Yarborough. It was the paint scheme Yarborough sported the day he and Donnie Allison clashed in the iconic 1979 Daytona 500.

As far as Most Popular Drivers: Petty won six of the ten titles in the decade, Allison won three, and Pearson the other one. All three would become series champions and easily make the NASCAR Hall of Fame. Considering their success throughout the 1970s, that seems entirely appropriate. After all, they had ruled the 1970s—a decade of change unlike any other.

David Pearson, seen here in 1979, won forty-seven Cup Series races in the 1970s, earning him the third-most victories behind Richard Petty (89) and Cale Yarborough (52). Over his twenty-eight seasons as a driver, Pearson recorded 105 wins—second to Richard Petty's 200 on the all-time wins list—in only 574 career starts.

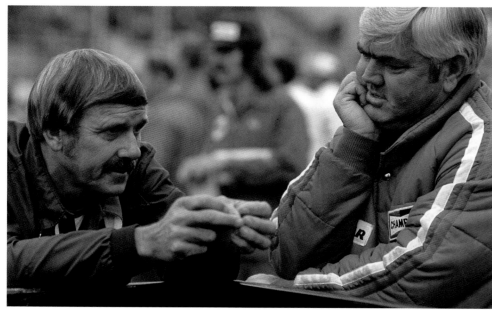

Legendary NASCAR team owner Junior Johnson (right) talks with crew chief and master mechanic "Suitcase" Jake Elder (left) before a race. One of the most colorful figures ever to grace a NASCAR garage, Elder was called "Suitcase" because it was said he always had his suitcase packed and ready to move to another team, which he did frequently throughout his career.

LEFT: **Race fans at the Alabama International Motor Speedway—now the Talladega Superspeedway—saw the Winston brand name every time they took a peek at the main infield scoreboard to see where their favorites were running in the race.**

BELOW: **From the start of NASCAR as an organization in 1949 until today, the Pettys have been a constant fixture at racetracks across the country. The family patriarch, Lee Petty (left) raced in the first NASCAR race ever run on June 14, 1949, at Charlotte Speedway. He went on to win fifty-four races over his sixteen-year career. Richard Petty's son Kyle (right) won eight races as a Cup Series driver over thirty years. Together, the Petty clan has gone to Victory Lane an incredible 262 times.**

BOBBY
ISAAC
(1970)

RICHARD
PETTY
(1971, 1972, 1974, 1975, 1979)

The 1970s began with Isaac, an Indigenous American from rural North Carolina, winning the Grand National title by 51 points over Bobby Allison. Led by legendary crew chief Harry Hyde, the No. 71 Dodge team owned by Nord Krauskopf won 11 of 47 starts and backed that with 21 more top-five finishes and six more top-tens. The team averaged starting 3.8th and finishing 6.8th. When Isaac abruptly retired midrace at Talladega in 1973, his career résumé showed 48 poles and 37 victories, 16 of them in the three-plus years he raced in the '70s.

Hyde, a decorated World War II combat veteran, once scoffed at the notion that their 1970 championship was cheapened because they won only on short tracks. "Why should it?" he said. "NASCAR made the schedule, we didn't. We showed up and raced where they told us to. Short track, long track, dirt, paved . . . it didn't matter to us. We're the champions, that's all that matters."

The eldest son of three-time champion Lee Petty was nearly unbeatable in his No. 43 cars during the '70s. With his brother, Maurice, and their cousin, Dale Inman, running the team, "the King" won 89 races and five of the decade's 10 Cup championships. In addition, he finished two more seasons as series runner-up and was top-five in points two other times. It's an unofficial record, but an impressive one just the same: nine top-five points finishes in a ten-year span.

Petty, who won almost every major race at least once, was involved in some of the decade's most spectacular finishes: the 1974 Firecracker 400, when leader David Pearson pulled over on the last lap, forcing Petty to pass, which allowed Pearson to draft past for the victory; the last-lap 1976 Daytona 500, when Petty and Pearson crashed running 1–2 in Turn 4 in arguably the sport's most famous finish; and the 1979 Daytona 500 that third-running Petty won after Donnie Allison and Yarborough wrecked each other out on the last lap.

BENNY PARSONS

(1973)

CALE YARBOROUGH

(1976, 1977, 1978)

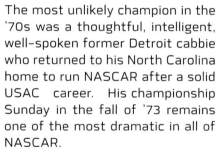

The most unlikely champion in the '70s was a thoughtful, intelligent, well-spoken former Detroit cabbie who returned to his North Carolina home to run NASCAR after a solid USAC career. His championship Sunday in the fall of '73 remains one of the most dramatic in all of NASCAR.

Parsons began the '70s winless in Cup, but was consistent enough to win the '73 title based on a Bristol victory, 15 top-five finishes, and 21 top tens in 28 starts. The drama? Parsons, the series leader, crashed out early in the season-finale at Rockingham, North Carolina. His hopes seemed crushed until crewmen from other teams helped get his No. 72 Chevrolet running again. He went back out and completed another 295 laps to finish 28th, good enough to beat Cale Yarborough by 67 points for the championship.

After winning 17 races with other teams early in the decade Yarborough and moonshiner-turned-racer-turned-owner Junior Johnson won 35 more in the '70s (then six more before separating in 1980). They won three consecutive titles, the first team to reach the "three-peat" milestone. (Their record stood unchallenged until future Hall of Fame driver Jimmie Johnson won five straight for Hendrick Motorsports between 2006 and 2010).

Unlike the Isaac-Hyde team that opened the decade, Yarborough and Johnson won on every type of track. Among them: the midlength speedways at Michigan, Rockingham, Darlington, Atlanta, and Charlotte; the super-speedways at Daytona Beach and Talladega; the short tracks at Bristol, Martinsville, Nashville, and North Wilkesboro; and the road course at Riverside. Seldom has a team been so dominant for so long as Yarborough–Johnson and their No. 11 Chevrolets during much of the decade.

95

Throughout the 1980s, a group of drivers including Buddy Arrington (67) competed week in and week out with the NASCAR "hot dogs" like Terry Labonte (44) and Dale Earnhardt (3), despite having virtually no chance to win. These "backmarkers" operated mostly on limited budgets, but still helped put on good shows at NASCAR tracks across the country. Many, like Arrington, who never even finished on the lead lap in 560 starts over twenty-five seasons, became fan favorites for their perseverance and dedication to the sport.

Chapter 4

THE 1980s

Reaching the Threshold of Speed

By Jimmy Creed

The distinct driving style of Dale Earnhardt, in which he liked to lean back and peer at the track right over the top of the steering wheel, served him well over the years. He was named Cup Series Rookie of the Year in 1979, won the 1980 Cup Series championship driving the yellow and blue No. 2 for Rod Osterlund, and went on to win a record-tying seven championships total. With Buddy Baker trailing, Earnhardt is seen here in 1980 at the Daytona 500, where he led many laps and suffered many disappointments before eventually winning the race in 1998.

FOR NASCAR, the decade of the 1980s was one highlighted by evolution, resolution, and the dominance of Darrell Waltrip.

It began with cars that, for the most part, were still truly "stock" cars. The kind that race fans could see on the track on Sunday and buy in the showroom on Monday. By its end, they had begun to evolve into the aerodynamic "marvels" seen today. Also near its end came the crash that changed NASCAR forever.

On Lap 21 of the 1987 Winston 500, at what was then known as the Alabama International Motor Speedway in Talladega, Alabama, Bobby Allison blew a right rear tire just as he came parallel with the jam-packed, front-stretch grandstand. The concussion lifted his Buick LeSabre's rear end in the air, spun it around and sent it hurtling backwards into the safety fencing, which was completely sliced open for approximately 50 feet by Allison's horrifying tumble.

Allison, luckily, walked away from the terrible crash and only a handful of spectators were injured, but the brush with utter disaster sent electric shocks surging throughout NASCAR and the entire racing world. At the time of the crash, Allison was traveling in a large pack of cars running approximately

ABOVE: **Before he became one of NASCAR's most recognizable team owners, Richard Childress was a journeyman driver who made 285 Cup Series starts over twelve seasons with a total of six top-five finishes to show for it. Seen here driving a No. 3 car at an unidentified race, his best career finish was third place in the 1978 Nashville 420 at Nashville Speedway.**

LEFT: **By his second full-time season on the Cup Series circuit, Dale Earnhardt (2) had already proven hard to handle, even for veterans like Richard Petty (43). Here Earnhardt races Petty in the Busch Volunteer 500 on August 23, 1980, at Bristol International Speedway. Earnhardt finished second in this race, two spots ahead of Petty, and went on to win his first Cup Series championship by the season's end.**

210 mph, and NASCAR's safety sultans resolved that never again would speeds approach those dangerous levels at Talladega and its sister track, the Daytona International Speedway.

When the 1988 Winston 500 rolled around, NASCAR had settled on restrictor plates—square aluminum metal pieces with four holes drilled in them—as its preferred safety measure. Placed between the carburetor and the intake manifold to reduce the flow of air and fuel into the engine's combustion chamber, the plates also reduced horsepower and, for better or worse depending on your perspective, have governed all things speed-related at Talladega and Daytona ever since.

And overall, there was Waltrip, who won more in the 1980s than any other driver not named Richard Petty or David Pearson did in any other decade in NASCAR history. Waltrip's fifty-seven trips to Victory Lane over that span tied him with Pearson, who won fifty-seven races in the 1960s and left him trailing only Petty, who posted an incredible 101 wins in the 1960s and eighty-nine wins in the 1970s.

Waltrip won nineteen races more than Dale Earnhardt, his nearest competitor, and the Winston Cup championships in 1981, 1982, and 1985 driving for Hall of Fame car owner Junior Johnson's juggernaut.

"There's no doubt it was a career-making move for Darrell," said Larry McReynolds, who began working in NASCAR in 1980 and served as a crew chief for the first time with rookie Mark Martin over the second half of the 1982 season. "He had won races with DiGard Racing, and was very successful, but when he went to that eleven car with Junior Johnson, it's like the magic switch really got flipped on."

Dale Earnhardt and Richard Childress first joined forces for eleven races in 1981, then parted ways again for two full seasons. But after teaming up full-time again in 1984, they formed one of the most dynamic duos in NASCAR Cup Series history. They won six championships and sixty-seven races across seventeen full seasons together before Earnhardt's death in 2001.

One of the most iconic photos in NASCAR history shows rookie Ron Bouchard (47) beating Darrell Waltrip (center) and Terry Labonte (far left) to the stripe by 2 feet to win the 1981 Talladega 500 on August 2. It was the only Cup Series win for the Fitchburg, Massachusetts, driver in 160 career starts at NASCAR's highest level, and still ranks as one of the closest finishes ever. Bouchard was voted the 1981 Cup Series Rookie of the Year.

ABOVE: **Neil Bonnett emerged as a racing force in the late 1970s, quickly becoming one of the most likable drivers on the Cup Series circuit. Bonnett took over the famed Wood Brothers No. 21 ride early in 1979 and won on only his third time out. Here he is joined by the Wood Brothers in Victory Lane at Dover Downs International Speedway after he drove the Woods' Mercury to victory in the CRC Chemicals 500 on September 20, 1981. Bonnett continued to drive for the Wood Brothers through the 1982 season and recorded nine of his eighteen career victories with them.**

THE WORLD'S FASTEST SPEEDWAY

For Waltrip, McReynolds, and all those in NASCAR at the time, the 1980s were dominated by the pursuit of speed, speed, and more speed, and the epicenter of that pursuit was the 2.66-mile layout in the east central Alabama countryside now known as the Talladega Superspeedway.

Over that span, the track was the site of NASCAR's first official 200-mph pole qualifying run, its first-ever all 200-mph field, and the setting of a record that will never be broken.

Benny Parsons was the first driver to record a 200-mph qualifying lap when he went 200.176 mph to win the pole for the 1982 Winston 500. He was also part of the forty-driver field that all qualified over 200 mph for the 1986 Winston 500, from Bill Elliott's 212.229 mph to win the pole to Jimmy Means's 202.563 mph in fortieth spot.

Finally, it was also Elliott who set the unbeatable mark of 212.809 mph to take the pole for the 1987 Winston 500—the same race that saw Allison's near miss and brought restrictor plates into the sport.

"I think the qualifying record at Talladega just kind of puts an exclamation point on our legacy," "Awesome Bill from Dawsonville" said in 2017. "I'm talking about our whole family—me, (brother) Dan, (brother) Ernie, and my dad. We came from a little town in Dawsonville, Georgia, that wasn't even on the map. We were kind of like David and Goliath with what we did and what we accomplished."

In taking the pole for the 1982 Winston 500 at what was then known as the Alabama International Motor Speedway, Benny Parsons became the first driver to record an official qualifying lap over 200 mph. Parsons posted a lap of 200.176 mph in his No. 28 J. D. Stacy–sponsored Pontiac.

LEFT: **After joining forces prior to the 1981 season, Darrell Waltrip (right) and Junior Johnson went on to form one of the most successful driver-owner duos in NASCAR history. Driving for Johnson for six seasons, Waltrip recorded consecutive Cup Series championships in 1981 and 1982 and won again in 1985. He also had second-place finishes in 1983 and 1986 and recorded forty-three victories in that span.**

ABOVE: **Darrell Waltrip dominated the 1982 season, taking over the championship from Bobby Allison en route to winning twelve races, including the Old Dominion 500 at Martinsville.**

"MILLION DOLLAR BILL" IS BORN

Another of Elliott's tremendous accomplishments was becoming the first driver to win the Winston Million in 1985. Series sponsor R. J. Reynolds Tobacco Company put up the prize for any driver who could win three of NASCAR's Big Four races—the Daytona 500, Talladega's Winston 500, Charlotte's Coca-Cola 600, and the Southern 500 at Darlington.

Elliott won the Daytona 500 in February 1985 and the Winston 500 in early May, but faltered with an eighteenth-place finish three weeks later at Charlotte. It meant he had to win the Southern 500 on September 1, 1985, and that chance appeared to have literally gone up in smoke when leader Cale Yarborough's power steering line failed, engulfing second-place Elliott and his No. 9 Ford Thunderbird in a thick, white plume in the track's fourth turn.

Somehow, Elliott emerged from the fog, took the lead, and sped to the checkers sixth-tenths of a second in front of Yarborough. In addition to the cool cash, the win earned him another catchy nickname—"Million Dollar Bill"—and another chapter in NASCAR lore.

"I AM THE WINSTON CUP CHAMPION"

In 1985 Bill Elliott won 11 superspeedway pole positions, 11 superspeedway races, and the first Winston Million prize ever put up by the R.J. Reynolds Tobacco Company. In fact he won practically everything there was to win in NASCAR that year except . . . the Winston Cup championship.

In an ironic twist, the driver who enjoyed one of the most successful seasons in NASCAR history did not win the sport's top honor that same year. Instead, in a testament to the scoring system created by long-time official statistician Bob Latford for the 1975 season that rewarded consistency over checkered flags, Darrell Waltrip took the title by an amazing 101 points.

Elliott actually led Waltrip by 206 points on September 1, 1985, but lost his grip on the top rung with a string of terrible finishes down the stretch.

"I can't complain," said Elliott, who finally won his only NASCAR championship in 1988. "We had a great year, and I don't know that I would trade any of it. We have a lot of years to run for the championship."

Waltrip, who won only four poles and three races, didn't shed any tears for Elliott after claiming his third and final championship.

"This year, I'm the beneficiary of the point system," said Waltrip, who earlier in the decade had said there was not enough incentive for winning races built into it. "I've been on the other end of it too. I will be the first to admit that with the year Bill has had, he deserves to be the champion. But we all knew the system and how it works at the beginning of the year and under this format, I earned the most points, and I am the Winston Cup champion."

"Awesome" Bill didn't receive any sympathy from the sanctioning body, either.

"We are happy with the current Winston Cup point formula," NASCAR Chief Executive Officer Bill France Jr. said. "The system works. In the last seven years, the Winston Cup championship has come down to the final race of the year. We think consistency is important in winning any championship.

"We do not subscribe to the theory that just because a certain driver wins the most races, he should automatically be the series champion. We feel we have a good point system, and we're going to keep it."

Which they did until finally instituting a playoff system starting with the 2004 season.

Darrell Waltrip (left) and Bill Elliott chat in the garage prior to the running of the 1985 Daytona 500.

Ricky Rudd's first race in Bud Moore's Wrangler Ford Thunderbird in 1984 ended up being much more exciting than he would have liked. In the season-opening Busch Clash at Daytona International Speedway, Rudd tumbled seven times after being bumped by Jody Ridley as they came off Turn 4 in a big pack of cars. Rudd suffered a concussion and a serious rib-cage injury in the crash that one commentator described as like "riding a bucking horse," but he toughed it out and drove in the Daytona 500 the next weekend with his eyes literally taped open with duct tape.

Ricky Rudd proved just how tough he was by driving the 1984 Daytona 500 with his eyes duct-taped open so he could see after being in a horrendous crash in the previous week's Busch Clash. Rudd finished seventh in the Daytona 500, then drove to victory the next week at the Richmond Fairgrounds Raceway with his eyes once again taped open. Despite getting busted up in Daytona, Rudd opened the 1984 season with seven straight top-ten finishes.

SOME RACES TO REMEMBER

It was one of several notable races during the decade etched in the history books and the memory banks of true NASCAR fans everywhere.

In the 1981 Talladega 500, as Waltrip and Terry Labonte battled each other coming off Turn 4, rookie Ron Bouchard pulled what was called a slingshot maneuver to beat them both to the line by less than 2 feet in what is still considered one of the closest finishes in NASCAR history. It was Bouchard's only victory in a 160-race NASCAR career, and afterwards the Fitchburg, Massachusetts, driver credited veteran racer and southerner Buddy Baker with giving him advice earlier in the week that helped him find Victory Lane.

"Well, I did have to listen pretty close a couple of times," Bouchard said with a laugh. "But when Buddy Baker speaks, you listen anyway."

PUNCH PACKED A PUNCH

Dr. Jerry Punch was a fixture on pit road and on television sets across the nation throughout the 1980s.

Punch, whose broadcasting career began in high school and who paid his way through North Carolina State with winnings earned by racing at local short tracks, received his medical degree from Wake Forest University School of Medicine in 1979. He would later work at Halifax Medical Center just down the street from Daytona International Speedway and even later serve as director of emergency medicine at a Palm Coast, Florida, hospital.

His two careers began to overlap when he first broadcasted NASCAR on the radio with Motor Racing Network starting in 1980. Then in 1984 ESPN hired him to be a pit road reporter.

Personable, knowledgeable, and well respected, Punch went on to add the Indianapolis 500, NASCAR play-by-play and college football sideline reporting to his considerable broadcasting résumé. He was also Jerry-on-the-spot at least twice on pit road.

On August 26, 1988, Punch watched as Rusty Wallace barrel rolled several times in a horrible crash at Bristol Motor Speedway. Punch reached the crumpled car before the track safety crews were even scrambled and found Wallace unconscious. Punch helped revive Wallace, who credits Punch with saving his life that day.

In November 1988, Punch was covering the Atlanta 500k ARCA Permatex Series race when driver Don Marmor crashed into another car that had veered into his way then hit a concrete barrier separating the track and pit road and overturned. Told that Marmor had died, Punch sprinted the length of pit road, climbed through the windshield opening and restarted Marmor's heart.

Marmor was unconscious for three weeks, in the hospital for over three months and never raced again. But he lived and served as one of several walking testaments to NASCAR and ESPN's good doctor.

Jerry Punch interviews Darrell Waltrip in the garage at Daytona Internatonal Speedway.

Geoff Bodine leads Bobby Allison and Richard Petty during the Sovran Bank 500 Cup race at Martinsville Speedway on April 29, 1984. It was the first victory in Bodine's nearly thirty-year Cup Series career, but even more importantly, it was the first Cup victory for his car owner, Rick Hendrick. The win helped keep the doors of Hendrick Motorsports open at a time when it looked like the racing operation was going to go under.

Another classic was the 1984 Firecracker 400 run on July 4, which fell on a Wednesday that year, at Daytona. It was iconic because it was the 200th and final coronation of "the King" Richard Petty and because there to crown him one final time was none other than President Ronald Reagan, who became the first sitting president ever to attend a NASCAR race in person.

Petty set the stage when he won the 199th race of his incredible career on May 20, 1984, at Dover Downs International Speedway, and over the next six weeks had four other opportunities to reach the 200-win mark. But as if from a script for a made-for-TV movie, Petty was still looking to top off his career win total with a nice, round number when he hit the sands and sweltering summer heat of Daytona on our nation's birthday.

Reagan, running for re-election that year, flew to Daytona in Air Force One and even gave the command for drivers to start their engines from there as he landed at a nearby airport. When it was complete and Petty had won a

hard-fought duel with Yarborough, he stopped at the Start/Finish line and went directly to the suite where Reagan had watched the race to receive congratulations from the president.

Reagan later joined Petty, and other NASCAR drivers, crew members, and their families in the Daytona garage area for a picnic at which Kentucky Fried Chicken and Pepsi—two of the sport's biggest sponsors at the time—were served and country singer Tammy Wynette sang her hit, "Stand by Your Man." The setting truly couldn't have been more American.

"With all the presidents that have ever been in the United States, this is the first one that ever showed up at a racetrack," Petty said in his postrace interview with ABC. "Everybody's got to go from that from a racing standpoint, and I wanted to be the one that was able to welcome him to Grand National racing."

Years later, Petty reflected that "the whole day, it was just beyond imagination."

Terry Labonte became known as NASCAR's "Ironman" by starting 655 consecutive races, a record that stood until 2002. He started all 296 Cup Series races run in the 1980s, including 87 from 1984 through 1986 in the Piedmont Airlines No. 44, seen here as Labonte battles with Darrell Waltrip.

Though Cale Yarborough (28) was a formidable foe all race long, Richard Petty managed to hold off him, Harry Gant, and several other NASCAR greats to record his record 200th career victory in the 1984 Firecracker 400. The July 4 crowd saw Yarborough lead seventy-nine laps to Petty's fifty-three. But when the race ended under caution, it was Petty who had made racing history in more ways than one.

Richard Petty sprays the crowd in Victory Lane with champagne after winning the 1984 Firecracker 400. It was the 200th and final victory in Petty's amazing thirty-five years as a Cup Series driver.

Another milestone race is one we've already touched on, the 1987 Winston 500. In addition to Elliott's all-time qualifying record and Allison's big wreck, the storyline was completed by Allison's son, Davey, recording his first career Winston Cup victory—and his dad miraculously being in Victory Lane to greet him.

After a two-and-a-half-hour delay while safety crews repaired the damaged catchfence, the rookie, making only his fourteenth career Winston Cup start, charged to the checkers, eventually leading 101 of the race's 179 laps (it was shortened by nine laps due to darkness.)

"We had the best engine in the business under that hood today," a beaming Davey said in Victory Lane. "That thing is so strong, I did anything I wanted to do."

On winning after seeing his father's terrible crash in his rearview mirror, Davey said he just had to keep concentrating on his driving.

"When I looked down and saw Dad bang into that wall, my heart sank way down," said Davey, who died in a helicopter crash in the Talladega infield in July 1993. "That is the worst crash I've ever seen, and it was my father. This was a day I went from the lowest low—when I saw that accident—to the highest high when I saw him get out of that car and walk away."

And then he found Victory Lane for the first time at this home track, to top it off.

"I've always wanted to win my first NASCAR race here," Davey said.

Finally, there was a race famous for a pass that wasn't really a pass in a race that wasn't really a race.

Richard Petty (left) and Bobby Allison (right) enjoy a picnic lunch with President Ronald Reagan after Petty won the 1984 Firecracker 400 on July 4, 1984, at the Daytona International Speedway. Reagan, who became the first sitting president to attend a live NASCAR race, called a few laps on the Motor Racing Network broadcast and visited with drivers, crew members, and their families in the garage afterwards.

"Awesome" Bill Elliott takes the checkered flag to win the 1985 Southern 500 at Darlington Raceway, earning a cool million dollars from R. J. Reynolds Tobacco Co. Elliott won the Daytona 500, the Winston 500 at Talladega, and the Southern 500 to take home the Winston Million bonus money, which had been offered to any driver who could win at least three of NASCAR's marquee four Cup Series races in a single season.

It came on May 17, 1987, in the Winston All-Star Race at Charlotte Motor Speedway and involved Earnhardt and Elliott.

Earnhardt came into the non-points-paying race first in the Winston Cup point standings and Elliott was second. Earnhardt had won six of the season's first nine races while Elliott had won the Daytona 500 and had a second and three fourths among the others. Earnhardt drove a Chevy and Elliott a Ford.

Also, Earnhardt's owner, Richard Childress, had an interesting philosophy on big money exhibition races like the Winston. He would tell "the Intimidator" to "bring me the trophy or bring me the steering wheel," and on this day he very nearly got both.

It was a rough race from the start, with Earnhardt, Elliott, and Geoff Bodine trading sheet metal so furiously that both Elliott and Earnhardt later accused the other of trying to wreck them intentionally. Then came the final ten-lap shootout and the dust really flew.

With $200,000 going to the winner, Elliott and Bodine started the final segment on the front row, and Earnhardt was fourth. As the cars went into Turn 1, Earnhardt shoved Bodine hard, and he lost control, slid down the track, and made contact with Elliott's right front. A spinning Bodine made additional contact with Elliott, and as he did, Earnhardt dove underneath both to take the lead.

On the next restart, Elliott set off in hot pursuit of Earnhardt, and with eight laps to go was giving as good as he was getting when Earnhardt turned almost completely sideways in front of Elliott coming off Turn 4. The move took both cars into the infield grass in the Charlotte tri-oval area, where Earnhardt eventually straightened out his yellow-and-blue Wrangler No. 3 and went on to claim the cash.

Even though it wasn't a pass, it became known as the "Pass in the Grass," and it is still one of NASCAR's most famous finishes. Plenty of feelings were hurt, though, and emotions were at a fever pitch on both sides afterwards.

"If a man has to run over you to beat you, it's time for this stuff to stop," an irate Elliott said postrace. "When a man pulls over and lets you by and then tries to run you into the wall, I'd say that was done deliberately. What he did wasn't right."

Understandably, Earnhardt had a different take on things.

"Bill and them got into it there and spun around and we just missed them, then I'll be darned if Bill tried to knock me out twice," Earnhardt said. "He had me sideways going off (Turn) 2 over there and then he turned me through the tri-oval. I didn't try to wreck him or run him into the wall or nothing. Then he tried to wreck me under the caution."

Then Earnhardt added with a sheepish grin, "I think he's a little upset."

Even a windshield that had to be taped into place couldn't keep Tim Richmond from Victory Lane in the 1986 Firecracker 400 at Daytona International Speedway. The victory came during a season in which he won seven times while driving for Hendrick Motorsports.

EARNHARDT, CHILDRESS TEAM UP

After winning Rookie of the Year honors in 1979, Earnhardt quickly served notice he was a new hired gun in town by winning the 1980 Winston Cup championship, the first of three in the decade (1986 and 1987 were the others) and a record-tying seven in his storied career.

Driving for owner Rod Osterlund, Earnhardt put his No. 2 Chevy in Victory Lane five times in 1980 and recorded nineteen top-five finishes and twenty-four top tens in thirty-one races to narrowly edge Yarborough for the title by nineteen points.

Despite the great start, less than a year later, just prior to the 1981 Firecracker 400, Osterlund sold the team to Kentucky businessman J. D. Stacy, who proudly proclaimed, "We are looking forward to a long and successful relationship with Dale Earnhardt, crew chief Dale Inman, and the Wrangler Racing team."

That "long" relationship lasted exactly four races and came to an end when journeyman racer Childress made a rash decision and pulled off one of the greatest coups in sports history.

Childress, who had mostly just made laps at NASCAR's highest level since 1969, didn't really want to quit driving his No. 3 car, but he knew Earnhardt was unhappy about his team being sold, and he saw an opportunity. It all came together over an August weekend at Talladega and was finalized in the Downtowner Hotel in nearby Anniston, Alabama.

Childress drove to a twenty-sixth-place finish and Earnhardt a twenty-ninth-place finish in the 1981 Talladega 500 on August 2, 1981, and it was the last time Childress ever got behind the wheel.

Bobby Allison's car comes to rest after his huge crash in the 1987 Winston 500 at Talladega that changed NASCAR forever. After a blown tire caused him to become airborne, Allison flew backwards towards a packed grandstand and took down a large section of catch fencing in the tri-oval area. A delay of 2 hours and 38 minutes was needed to make repairs to the fence before the race could be restarted. Following the restart, Allison's son Davey went to Victory Lane for the first time in his Cup Series career. As a result of the crash, restrictor plates would become a staple safety measure in the sport.

NASCAR AND TV . . . A GREAT MARRIAGE

With the success of CBS's first-ever live, flag-to-flag coverage of the 1979 Daytona 500, NASCAR embraced television and by 1985, every race on the then-Winston Cup schedule was shown in some form or fashion.

In those early days, networks cut deals with individual track owners instead of NASCAR as a whole, making for a jumble of call letters and broadcasters across a myriad of stations. ABC, NBC, ESPN, the Nashville Network (TNN), and WTBS were just some of those that dove into NASCAR in the 1980s—but for any fan willing to search, the content was there.

ESPN aired its first race March 1, 1981, a tape-delayed broadcast of the Carolina 500 from Rockingham, and its first live broadcast was the Atlanta Journal 500 on November 11, 1981. The cable network emerged as the major player in the 1980s, broadcasting 65 of the 191 total races that were aired during the decade.

The folks in front of the cameras were some of NASCAR's most famous or would become some of the sport's most famous personalities through their work on television.

Ken Squier, who did the play-by-play of the iconic 1979 Daytona 500, the late Bob Jenkins, and long-time Fox point man Mike Joy became the voices synonymous with NASCAR during this era, but others such as Al Michaels and even the legendary Keith Jackson took turns calling races as well. In fact, it was Jackson on the call for the 1987 The Winston all-star race at Charlotte when the famous "Pass In The Grass" incident took place between winner Dale Earnhardt and Bill Elliott.

Among the dozens of color commentators, the various networks also employed many beloved former NASCAR drivers including Buddy Baker, Benny Parsons, and Ned Jarrett who became household fixtures as broadcasters as well.

The networks also quickly began experimenting with in-car cameras and radios that allowed on-track interviews with drivers, technology that has evolved into staples of modern-day coverage.

Altogether it was a hodgepodge of ingredients mixed into a magic potion that worked to help lay the groundwork for the incredible television coverage NASCAR now receives from its network partners.

By 1989 almost all races were broadcast live, and by 2001 NASCAR had negotiated a $2.4 billion rights fee deal with Fox and NBC as television broadcast partners and FX and TBS (later TNT) as cable television broadcast partners, which included complete coverage of what are now the Xfinity Series and Camping World Truck Series that continues to this day.

ABC Sports crewmembers cover a race. NASCAR and television made for a great marriage after CBS's exciting flag-to-flag coverage of the 1979 Daytona 500.

Though he had no way of knowing it at the time, Bill Elliott set a record that will never be broken when he went 212.809 mph to win the pole for the 1987 Winston 500 at Talladega on July 26, after which he posed for this photo in Victory Lane. Following a terrible crash by Bobby Allison during the race, NASCAR mandated restrictor plates to control speeds at Talladega Superspeedway and Daytona International Speedway, meaning that Elliott's one-lap qualifying record for a NASCAR Cup race will never again be threatened.

Two weeks later at Michigan International Speedway, Earnhardt and the Wrangler-sponsorship–adorned Childress' No. 3 Pontiac, and NASCAR's ultimate power duo was unveiled—one that would win sixty-seven races and six championships together before Earnhardt's death at the end of the 2001 Daytona 500, on February 18, 2001.

The move was a huge gamble for Childress, however, as he had to take out a second mortgage on his house and risk almost everything, so he had just to get a deal with Earnhardt that was only good for the last eleven races of the 1981 season.

The two again went their separate ways after that season, with Earnhardt going to renowned owner Bud Moore and his iconic No. 15 Ford for 1982 and 1983 while Childress went with Ricky Rudd as he sought even more financial stability for his young Richard Childress Racing team. But when they reunited in 1984, Earnhardt would never again drive a car without a "3" on its side.

"When Osterlund was bought out by J. D. Stacy, Dale didn't want to be sold was basically what it boiled down," Childress recounted to Fox Sports years later. "I didn't want to get out of the car, but I knew the opportunity was there—and I didn't want to pass up what was a great opportunity. I knew Dale was a championship driver. That was one of the biggest breaks in the history of RCR and for Richard Childress."

It was one of the biggest for NASCAR as well.

SEVERAL NEW LEGENDS EMERGE

Earnhardt was among a sizable group of NASCAR Hall of Famers or future Hall of Famers who emerged as the sport's dominant forces in the 1980s and left indelible marks on it forever.

In addition to Allison, future Winston Cup champions Rusty Wallace, Alan Kulwicki, and Dale Jarrett, and other notable drivers such as Martin and the flamboyant Tim Richmond, all ran their first career races in the 1980s.

In particular, Wallace made an incredible splash when he came home second to Earnhardt in his first race, the 1980 Atlanta 500, at the then Atlanta International Raceway.

Kulwicki debuted in 1985 and won his first race in 1988. That came in the first NASCAR Winston Cup race ever run at Phoenix International Raceway, and Kulwicki made it even more memorable by breaking out the "Polish Victory Lap," circling the track backwards with the checkered flag so he could acknowledge the fans more easily through his driver-side window. He displayed it four more times before he died in a plane crash as he flew to Bristol International Speedway for a race in early April 1993.

BELOW: **A technician checks a carburetor restrictor plate before it is installed on a NASCAR Cup engine. The plate restricts the flow of air-fuel mixture to the engine, thus reducing speeds, and has been mandated by NASCAR as a safety measure at Talladega Superspeedway and Daytona International Speedway ever since Bobby Allison almost flew into the grandstands in a terrible crash during the 1987 Winston 500 at Talladega.**

LEFT: **Bobby Allison, driver of the No. 12 Miller High Life Buick, and son Davey, driver of the No. 28 Texaco Havoline Ford, finished first and second in the 1988 Daytona 500. It was the second of two Daytona 500 wins for Bobby Allison, and it came on Valentine's Day.**

Then there was Richmond, who came from Indy Car racing in 1980 and became an instant fan favorite.

With *GQ* model looks and a rock-star air about him, Richmond seemed to come straight from Central Casting to play the part of a NASCAR race car driver. In fact, it is widely believed that the characters played by Tom Cruise and Robert Duvall in the 1990 racing movie *Days of Thunder* were loosely based on Richmond and his long-time crew chief, Harry Hyde.

He could drive, too, and eventually won thirteen races over parts of eight seasons in NASCAR, including seven wins in 1986. But Richmond fell ill the day after the annual NASCAR Awards Banquet in New York that December and, despite a lengthy stay in a Cleveland hospital, was not well enough to begin the 1987 season.

Suffering from what was reported as pneumonia, Richmond missed the first twelve races of 1987 before making a spectacular return by winning at Pocono and Riverside in his first two races back. He ran six more times, but after finishing twenty-ninth in the Champion Spark Plug 400 at Michigan International Speedway on August 16, 1987, he was gone from the sport for good.

Richmond died on August 19, 1989, at thirty-four years old, and ten days later his family held a press conference to confirm that the cause was complications from AIDS.

Bobby Allison (right) and Davey Allison share a moment in Victory Lane after the elder Allison captured victory in the 1988 Daytona 500 NASCAR Cup race. Davey Allison finished second to his dad in the race.

HENDRICK HANGS ON . . . BARELY

Richmond posted nine of his career victories for NASCAR Hall of Fame car owner Rick Hendrick, who entered the sport in 1984 hoping to "someday win one race." But early on that season, the chances looked bleak. In fact Hendrick, whose team had no sponsor, told his crew chief, Hyde, if they didn't get a good finish in the 1984 Transouth 500 at Darlington on April 15, 1984, it was probably over.

Bodine crashed on lap 107 and finished thirty-fifth that day, and Hendrick was ready to focus on selling cars full-time. But Hyde wasn't ready to give up without one more fight.

"Harry was a great salesman," Hendrick recalled. "He kept saying, 'Just let us go to Martinsville. Bodine is good there. We can win.' He talked me into it. We won the race and ended up getting a sponsor because of it. The rest is history."

Bodine did indeed win the 1984 Sovran Bank 500 to record his first career victory and save Hendrick Motorsports in the process. Ironically, Hendrick wasn't at Martinsville to see his saving race as he and his wife had chosen to attend a church retreat that weekend instead. So he had to call his momma to learn his racing fate.

"I called her from a pay phone and asked about the race. She said, dead seriously, 'You haven't heard? He blew up,'" Hendrick said. "I thought it was all over. Then she said, 'No, he won!' I couldn't believe it; I about dropped the phone. Then we went straight to Bodine's house (near Greensboro, North Carolina) and covered his yard in toilet paper. It was such a relief to win. If we hadn't, there's no way we'd be here today."

Alan Kulwicki turns laps en route to victory in the 1988 Checker 500 at Phoenix International Raceway on November 6. It was the first Cup Series race ever run at the one-mile facility in the desert, and it was also the first of five victories in Kulwicki's Cup Series career.

Driving Raymond Beadle's No. 27 Kodiak Pontiac Grand Prix, Rusty Wallace scored six wins and twenty top-ten finishes to win his only Cup Series championship in 1989. In one of the tightest championship battles in NASCAR history, Wallace edged out Dale Earnhardt Sr. by just twelve points to take the title.

BACK MARKERS MAKE THEIR MARK

As Hendrick and others grew into NASCAR icons in the 1980s, there was also a group of drivers known as back markers or field fillers who became fan favorites for their efforts in the face of continued futility.

There was J. D. McDuffie, who drove in an incredible 653 races over parts of twenty-seven seasons without ever once finishing on the lead lap. McDuffie died in a crash at Watkins Glen on August 11, 1991.

There was also Buddy Arrington, who ran 560 races without finishing on the lead lap, and Means, who appropriately enough was once sponsored by Alka-Seltzer, who ran 455 career races with only three lead laps finishes. Those and many others like them raced in relative anonymity, but they loved the sport just as much as the front runners like Waltrip and company did.

OL' D. W. DROVE TOO

Oh yes, Waltrip, the driver Johnson once described as, "that mouthy little ole boy over in Tennessee." Of course, when he said it in the summer of 1973, Johnson was responding to a question from reporters about who he foresaw as NASCAR's future stars.

"I don't think there's any doubt about it," Johnson recalled telling the reporters in his book *Brave for Life Junior Johnson*. "I think it's going to be Ralph Earnhardt's boy and that mouthy little ole boy over in Tennessee. What's his name? Waltrip. Yeah, that mouthy Waltrip."

"Ol' D. W." proved Johnson correct, winning eighty-four career races—tied for fourth with Bobby Allison on NASCAR's all-time wins list—then went on to a nineteen-year career as lead analyst on Fox Sport's NASCAR broadcasts before retiring from that after the 2019 season. In that capacity, he was more popular than he probably ever was as a driver.

"I get more mail today than I've ever gotten in my life," Waltrip told NASCAR. com. "But here's the thing: a lot of people don't know that I ever drove. It's amazing to me the number of people that think all I've ever done is TV, and I'm only famous for saying 'Boogity, Boogity, Boogity, Let's Go Racin' Boys.'"

The man who won seven straight races at Bristol Motor Speedway from 1981 to 1984 admits that during his racing career such an oversight would have bothered him, but not now.

"In actuality, I think it's a great opportunity for me to share what I've done in my career as a driver, my career as a broadcaster and TV," Waltrip said. "I've written books, I've traveled with and known presidents and governors, and our car business is going great, we sell more cars than we ever have. I've just done a lot of things."

All in great part thanks to his historic run in the 1980s.

A WAKEUP CALL

As a historian of the sport, McReynolds can certainly recall and appreciate the achievements and milestones of Waltrip and many others over what was his first decade in the sport. He also fondly recollects his own personal accomplishments in that span, like his first full-time crew job with Kenny Bernstein's No. 26 Quaker State team and Joe Ruttman in 1986, and his first career victory as a crew chief with Rudd in that same car at Watkins Glen in 1988.

But his most vivid memory, and the one that all of NASCAR should always appreciate most, he said, is that of a catchfence doing what it was supposed to on a scorching hot July day in Talladega, Alabama.

"It was the unfortunate wakeup call that we had to keep the cars under 200 mph," McReynolds said. "Honestly, if Bobby Allison gets up in the grandstand that day, I don't know where the sport would be today. Fortunately, Bobby didn't get hurt, and we didn't have any fans that were seriously injured or killed.

"It was the wakeup call that told us racing is about speed, but there is a threshold, and we always have to keep that in mind."

Tim Richmond (center) was one of the most talented drivers ever to race in NASCAR, and though his star burned out way too soon, he is remembered as one of NASCAR's best. Richmond is shown here in Victory Lane after one of his thirteen Cup Series victories with veteran NASCAR chief Harry Hyde. It is widely believed that the relationship between the two served as the inspiration for the Tom Cruise and Robert Duvall characters in the 1990 racing movie *Days of Thunder*. Richmond passed away in 1989.

DALE EARNHARDT
(1980, 1986, 1987)

DARRELL WALTRIP
(1981, 1982, 1985)

BOBBY ALLISON
(1983)

CHAMPS

"The Intimidator" followed up a Rookie of the Year winning season in 1979 by winning the first of his seven career championships—a mark that tied him with Richard Petty for the most in NASCAR history—in 1980. The son of NASCAR legend Ralph Earnhardt, his 1986 and 1987 wins were the most dominant of the decade as he won by 288 points over runner-up Waltrip in 1986 and a whopping 489 over 1987 runner-up Bill Elliott. The father of Dale Earnhardt Jr. won 76 races in his 27-year career before being killed in a last-lap crash in the 2001 Daytona 500.

Brash, cocky, and arrogant were often used to describe ol' D. W. in the 1980s, but winner was another term for him as well. He won 12 races each in taking the 1982 and 1983 titles in tight duels with Bobby Allison, then took the 1985 title over Bill Elliott despite trailing Elliott 11-3 in the win column. In fact, Elliott led Waltrip by 206 points on September 1, 1985, yet Waltrip surged past him over the season's last nine races to claim the crown by 101 points. Waltrip posted 84 wins in a 29-year career, tying him with Allison for fourth on NASCAR's all-time wins list.

The leader of the famed "Alabama Gang" was runner up in the championship Chase five times before finally claiming his only career title in 1983. Less than five years later, he was out of the sport following a terrible crash at Pocono in June 1988 that put him in a coma for 108 days and robbed him of many of his greatest racing memories. He claims an 85th career victory, a 1971 win at Bowman Gray Stadium which would break the tie with Waltrip, that for some reason NASCAR has never officially given him credit for.

TERRY LABONTE

(1984)

BILL ELLIOTT

(1988)

RUSTY WALLACE

(1989)

"Texas" Terry posted just two wins, on the short track at Bristol and the road course at Riverside, but still outpointed Harry Gant by 65 to earn his first of two championships. In winning his second championship in 1996, he again won just two races, on the short track at North Wilkesboro and, finally, on a superspeedway at Charlotte. Besides his driving ability, Terry's other claim to fame was his durability. He set a then-NASCAR record by driving in every race run from January 14, 1979, through July 23, 2000—a string of 655 straight.

It took a while, but "Awesome Bill from Dawsonville" finally bounced back from his 1985 disappointment by winning his only title in 1988, squeezing past Rusty Wallace by a mere 24 points. Bill wasn't nearly as dominant in 1988, winning six races, the same number as Wallace. But he was good enough. Perhaps most importantly to current fans, Bill met his wife, Cindy, mother of Chase, at a photo shoot during the 1988 season, and the two were married in 1992.

Rusty rounded out an era in which every champion would be inducted into the NASCAR Hall of Famer by squeaking past Earnhardt by a paper-thin 12 points. It was the third slimmest margin of victory in the 29 years NASCAR used the scoring system it instituted in 1975, trailing only Alan Kulwicki (10 points in 1992) and Richard Petty (11 points in 1979). Wallace recorded 55 victories in his 26-year career, putting him 11th on NASCAR's all-time list. At his retirement in 2005, the 1984 Rookie of the Year had driven in 697 straight races, which currently stands fourth on the all-time list.

In the 1990s, NASCAR was, in many ways, the tale of Jeff Gordon and Dale Earnhardt. Here the two confer on race day for the Tyson Holly Farms 400 in North Wilkesboro, North Carolina, on September 29, 1996. Gordon won the race while the veteran Earnhardt finished second.

Chapter 5

THE 1990s

Earnhardt and Gordon Drive the Sport Forward

By Mike Hembree

Harry Gant celebrates winning the Heinz Southern 500 at Darlington Raceway on September 1, 1991. It was the first of four straight races in which Gant drove the No. 33 Skoal Bandit Oldsmobile to victory. After Darlington, Gant won at Richmond, Dover, and Martinsville in succession, posting a career high of five victories overall that season.

NASCAR IN THE 1990s featured the tale of two drivers—one a veteran at the peak of his skills and success, the other a youngster riding a rocket that, once launched, would rule NASCAR skies for years: Dale Earnhardt and Jeff Gordon.

Earnhardt won his fourth Cup championship in 1990 and added number five a year later. Championships six and seven would follow in 1993 and 1994 as he tied Richard Petty for the Cup's all-time championship total. The assumption at that stage was that Earnhardt, who had totaled fifty-three Cup victories at the time of Petty's retirement in 1992, eventually would break the King's record of seven titles.

That was not to be, but it was one of the few major accomplishments Earnhardt failed to attain.

Building on the aggressive driving style he had shown since his early years in the sport, Earnhardt breezed through much of the 1990s as NASCAR's top dog, a fan favorite who had used his rough-and-tumble approach to racing and his North Carolina mill-hill roots to become a runaway commercial success. His black caps and T-shirts dominated the grandstands, and Earnhardt tattoos—on the arms of men (and other body parts of women)—could be seen at practically every schedule stop. An Earnhardt fan from Pennsylvania inked most of his back with a design featuring Earnhardt's head and race car.

Andy Petree was crew chief for Earnhardt at Richard Childress Racing from 1993 to 1995, a span that produced two championships and fifteen race wins. Petree saw The Man up close and often watched in disbelief at some of Earnhardt's on-track magic.

"The biggest thing he had was so much confidence," Petree said. "Even if he wasn't the fastest, he had so many other methods, we might say, to be able to beat his competitors.

LEFT: **Davey Allison (center) celebrates in victory lane at Daytona International Speedway with crew chief Larry McReynolds (left), and car owner Robert Yates, (right) after winning the 1992 Daytona 500. The trio was the backbone of one of NASCAR's strongest racing organizations in the late 1980s and early 1990s.**

BELOW: **Davey Allison on his way to winning the 1992 Daytona 500 at Daytona International Speedway on February 16, 1992. A fan favorite during its run in the late 1980s and early 1990s, Allison's Texaco Havoline paint scheme is still considered one of the most iconic in NASCAR history to this day.**

"Back then, you could take a car that was not as good as the others and overcome it. He was really good at that. I can go back through my notes from then, and I tried to give an honest assessment after every race. There were times when we didn't have the best car, but he figured out how to beat them. I have a lot of notes like that."

Earnhardt critics are quick to voice the opinion that he often won races not so much by his skills but by his spills. He drove hard into corners, eating up brakes and shadowing those in front of him. He wasn't shy about popping the rear of a car in front to create space for a pass, and he was involved in more than a few on-track "disagreements" over the years, even with drivers who were among his best friends.

Two of Earnhardt's most notable on-track altercations occurred at the same venue—Bristol Motor Speedway—and involved the same driver, Terry Labonte, ironically one of Earnhardt's hunting buddies. Known for its fast, tight racing and postrace pit-road drama after driver versus driver confrontations, Bristol was the perfect place for a brouhaha involving Earnhardt.

On the final lap of the 1995 Goody's 500 at BMS, Labonte led Earnhardt by inches. Earnhardt bumped Labonte, a smart and patient driver who rarely was involved in controversy and pushed him into the outside wall. Labonte regained control of his sliding, damaged car and crossed the finish line first to win the race, marking a strange moment for any driver—being challenged by Earnhardt and hanging on for victory.

In the same race four years later, again under the lights at Bristol, Labonte passed Earnhardt for the lead before the pair took the white flag signifying the last lap. Earnhardt quickly returned the favor, bumping Labonte into the first-turn wall and regaining the lead. This time Labonte couldn't recover. Earnhardt swept to the victory, with Labonte finishing eighth, a lap down because of the accident. Surprisingly, many in the packed grandstands booed Earnhardt as he climbed from his car in victory lane, an uncommon rebuke for one of the sport's all-time fan favorites at a track where he was widely adored.

Those were two tough races, Earnhardt winning one and not the other. There were many other race days when he cruised to wins, making success look like elementary school math. One of those races was the 1995 Goody's 500 at Martinsville Speedway. He led 253 of the 500 laps and won with relative ease, even seeming to relax behind the wheel over the race's second half, cruising around the 0.5-mile track as if he was on a Sunday drive.

"Lap after lap he's leading the race, and I look up and he has his right arm on the roll bar (stretched out) and the other arm on the steering wheel," Petree said. "I'm like, 'What the hell? What are you doing? Why are you doing that?'" He said, 'Because I could.' I think he used it to relieve some of the physical stress. He kind of got comfortable doing that."

Despite a career filled with every kind of success imaginable, Earnhardt faced the devil at the start of every season. The Daytona 500, easily NASCAR's

THIS SPREAD: **The 1992 Hooters 500 season finale at Atlanta Motor Speedway is considered by many to be the greatest NASCAR race of all time as three major storylines played out in that one event. It was the 1,184th and final race of Richard Petty's thirty-five-year NASCAR career and the first career Winston Cup start for Jeff Gordon. During this race, driver and owner Alan Kulwicki won a shootout with six other drivers to claim his only career Winston Cup championship with a second-place finish.**

Alan Kulwicki hoists the 1992 Winston Cup Series trophy after clinching it in the Hooters 500 at Atlanta Motor Speedway on November 15, 1992. Kulwicki was the last driver and owner to win a Cup Series championship. Less than five months later, he was killed in a plane crash while flying to Bristol Motor Speedway to prepare for that week's Cup Series race.

biggest race, opened the schedule, and its victory lane seemed closed forever to Earnhardt, who "lost" the race in myriad dramatic ways over the years.

The most painful came in 1990. Earnhardt held a comfortable lead taking the white flag, and his legion of fans stood and cheered across Daytona's sweeping grandstands, anticipating the black No. 3 Chevrolet finally winning the 500. But Earnhardt ran over a piece of debris on the backstretch, causing a tire to explode. He slowed, and second-place Derrike Cope, a journeyman driver with no Cup victories, inherited the win, scoring one of the biggest upsets in NASCAR history. Earnhardt grumbled after the race that maybe he wasn't meant to win the 500.

It took eight more years for him to solve the puzzle. He finally won the 500 in 1998, sparking a celebration for the ages. In an unusual salute, crew members from every competing team lined up along pit road to shake Earnhardt's hand as he drove slowly to victory lane. Later, arriving in the press box to discuss the race, he tossed a toy monkey into the air and proclaimed, "Now that monkey's off my back!"

It had been a twenty-year quest.

A week later, still buoyed by the win, Earnhardt walked up to Dale Inman, Richard Petty's long-time crew chief, in the North Carolina Motor Speedway garage. "After Dale won, at the race at Rockingham the next week he came by and grabbed me by the cheek," Inman said. "He said, 'I can whip you now. I've won the 500.' I said, 'And you're six behind.'"

Petty won the 500 seven times.

Jeff Gordon, who would score on NASCAR's high ground in the 500 at Daytona three times (1997, 1999, 2005), arrived in stock car racing having taken a major detour from his imagined career path.

Gordon started racing on California short tracks in quarter-midget cars as a five-year-old. He rapidly showed promise, and his stepfather, John Bickford, moved the family to Indiana when Gordon was thirteen so he would have access to racing opportunities not available to youngsters in California. It was a decision that proved golden for Gordon, who soon became a star in United States Auto Club midget- and sprint-car racing. He seemed on target to advance to the higher levels of open-wheel racing and eventually arrive in the IndyCar series, but, with major-league open-wheel racing in a period of struggle and with NASCAR riding an upward curve, Gordon and his family took an exit toward stock cars.

After training at former NASCAR driver Buck Baker's driving school at North Carolina Motor Speedway, Gordon joined NASCAR's second-level Busch Series for a nearly full-season run in 1991. He scored three wins on that tour in 1992 and caught the eye of Cup Series team owner Rick Hendrick, who signed Gordon and paired him with young crew chief Ray Evernham, who would revolutionize standard approaches to pit and race strategy. Hendrick rose in the sport alongside his new driver, as the automobile dealership owner brought a new and vibrant approach to the concept of multi-car teams. For many years, drivers generally had rejected the idea of "teammates," but Hendrick proved the process could work and, by the mid-1990s, other top owners were following his lead. Before the decade ended, Hendrick's operation, which began in 1984 with five employees, had more than 500.

ALL-STAR SPECTACLE

Over the years, NASCAR's annual All-Star Race for the Cup Series has had highs and lows, great finishes and runaways, controversy and calm.

In 1992, the race was a spectacle unlike any before or since. The hype entering the all-star event was boiling, thanks in large part to the promotional genius of Humpy Wheeler, the Charlotte Motor Speedway executive who took racing public relations to a new level.

His idea for the '92 version of the All-Star Race was off the wall. To add new fire to the event, Wheeler had this thought: Why not run it at night?

Wait a minute . . . a NASCAR superspeedway race at night? High speeds and tight competition after dark? Sure there were Cup night races at short tracks, but would that environment work at a big track?

Wheeler brought in lighting experts who, after some study and investigation, said lighting the racing surface and pit road could be accomplished with a unique mirror system that brightened the speedway but kept lights from the drivers' eyes.

The system was constructed, and a test session scheduled prior to the race verified that it would work. Drivers ran dozens of test laps and said racing on the high-speed surface at night would not be a problem. "It was just like daylight," one driver said.

Wheeler promoted the race as "One Hot Night," and anticipation built as the May 16 date approached.

The result was all that Wheeler and NASCAR could have wanted. Dale Earnhardt, Kyle Petty, and Davey Allison were racing for the win on the final lap. On the backstretch, Petty tried to take the lead from Earnhardt, who dropped low in an attempt to block Petty's advance. Petty drove onto the track apron, and when he returned to the main groove Earnhardt lost control of his car and slid through the third turn.

Petty, recovering from his duel with Earnhardt, drove a bit high into Turn 4 and opened the door slightly for Allison, who was charging hard from second. Allison muscled his way into the lead as they approached the checkered flag, and he won the race by a few feet. The two cars collided after the finish, sending Allison's Ford sailing into the wall.

Safety workers had to cut into Allison's damaged car to remove him. He missed victory lane and spent the night in a Charlotte area hospital.

The race proved that big-track night racing was not only possible but profitable. Other speedways rushed to light their tracks, and even giant Daytona International Speedway eventually joined the push.

Wheeler's idea changed the sport in a big way, especially in the realm of the television networks, which enjoyed the opportunity to set start times later in the day for finishes during prime-time viewing hours.

On May 16, 1992, Charlotte Motor Speedway hosted the first race ever run at night on a superspeedway. The event was billed as "One Hot Night," and it did not disappoint. Davey Allison won the race, but celebrated his victory from a hospital bed. After a very tight race to the finish line, second-place finisher Kyle Petty clipped Allison and sent him crashing hard into the front stretch wall. The incident sent an unconscious Allison to the hospital, where he was kept overnight for observation.

ABOVE LEFT: **Fans at Pocono International Raceway display homemade banners honoring the late Davey Allison during the Miller Genuine Draft 500 on July 18, 1993. The race was the first Cup event to be run after Allison died on July 13, 1993, from injuries suffered in a helicopter crash while trying to land in the Talladega Superspeedway infield.**

ABOVE RIGHT: **Dale Jarrett (18) takes the checkered flag just ahead of Dale Earnhardt (3) and Geoff Bodine (15) in the Daytona 500 by STP at Daytona International Speedway, on February 15, 1993. It was the first of Jarrett's four Daytona 500 victories. The win was made even more memorable for race fans watching at home as Jarrett's father, NASCAR legend Ned Jarrett, called the final lap on the CBS television broadcast of the race, rooting his son on to victory.**

Gordon emerged into stardom in 1994 as NASCAR challenged other top-level sports—the National Football League, National Basketball Association, Major League Baseball—for media and fan attention. The NASCAR schedule expanded to new markets during the decade, and older speedways added grandstands to meet spectator demand. It became standard at many races to see ticket scalpers offering tickets for much more than their printed value. Television ratings soared, and, in mid-decade, *Sports Illustrated*, in a cover story, declared NASCAR "America's Hottest Sport."

NASCAR made its debut on one of racing's hallowed grounds—Indianapolis Motor Speedway—in 1994, and Gordon, who had built his racing résumé in Indiana, won the first Brickyard 400 August 6. A crowd of more than 300,000 streamed into IMS that day, setting a NASCAR attendance record, and many were screaming Gordon's name as he crossed the finish line.

Two months earlier, Gordon had scored his first Cup victory, surviving NASCAR's marathon race, the Coca-Cola 600 at Charlotte, to cross the finish line first. As fireworks exploded over the speedway, Gordon wept in victory lane. He would drive on to claim his first of four Cup championships in 1995, winning seven races and, at twenty-four, becoming the youngest champion of the modern era.

Gordon would evolve into much more than a motorsports superstar. Young, handsome, and well-spoken, he brought a new dynamic to stock car racing, and his style and success attracted new and different sponsors and carried the sport into new territory. He hosted the popular *Saturday Night Live* television show and made numerous other appearances in media generally closed to NASCAR in previous years.

Ironically Gordon was largely an afterthought in his first Cup race. That would be the November 15, 1992, Hooters 500 at Atlanta Motor Speedway, the finale of that season.

It became a day unlike any other in NASCAR history. Several rivers were merging into one. One of the sport's closest championship battles would be decided by the end of the day. Several drivers started the race with a shot at the big money.

Gordon, twenty-one, buckled into a Cup car for the first time. He started twenty-first and finished thirty-first, parking his Chevrolet halfway through the race after crashing. Few people could imagine how the arc of his time as a Cup driver would develop from that point.

The biggest piece of the puzzle that day at Atlanta involved Richard Petty, the sport's king and the man who had been at the center of stock car racing—in one way or another—for much of his life and much of the sport's life. It finally had come down to this—one final race, one more green, one more checkered. Petty, now fifty-five, had been racing in NASCAR's top series since 1958. It was time—past time, really, he would admit—to make the final turn.

Donnie Allison, Davey Allison's uncle, drives a memorial lap before the DieHard 500 at Talladega Superspeedway in honor of his nephew, who died on July 13, 1993, from injuries suffered in a helicopter crash at the track. Donnie drove the car that Davey had planned to race in that day. Donnie Allison said it was the hardest lap he ever drove in a racecar.

Pittsboro, Indiana, native Jeff Gordon leads Sterling Marlin into Turn 1 at the famed Indianapolis Motor Speedway during the inaugural NASCAR Brickyard 400 run on August 6, 1994. Gordon crossed the stripe .53 seconds ahead of Brett Bodine to record the second victory in his Hall of Fame career.

The weekend was filled with Petty salutes. It was the end of a year of tributes, Petty having declared his final season a Fan Appreciation Tour. Small diecast cars marking his last appearance at each track were rushed to market, and they flowed across the sales counters. The band Alabama sang his praises in a tribute concert on the last weekend. Atlanta Motor Speedway was jammed for Petty's 1,184th race.

Prior to the race, in the drivers meeting, Petty was saluted by his peers, and he gave each of the other drivers in the starting lineup a silver money clip with an engraving—"Thanks for all the memories, Richard Petty."

"My dad lived in a construction trailer as a kid," said Kyle Petty, Richard's son and a third-generation driver in a family that would put four generations in race cars. "A wooden construction trailer. They were dead dirt poor. Then they found out you could race and win 150 bucks. My god, thought my grandfather, I can feed the family for a month with that. Richard Petty and his life evolved from that. He changed as soon as he wasn't able to get back in a car again. Part of who Richard Petty was—he had to take that and put it in a box and put it on a shelf. That part of what he was is in a museum and in his house."

And the sport raced on.

Terry Labonte and the Kellogg Company had one of the longest driver-sponsor relationships in NASCAR history. From 1994 to 2004, some form of the Kellogg's paint scheme adorned Labonte's car, covering 368 races over eleven full seasons.

CANCELED FLIGHT

In the early 1990s, a disturbing trend developed in Cup racing. Cars thought they could fly.

It happened far too often, particularly at the tour's biggest tracks. For one reason or another, and at unpredictable moments, race cars lifted into the air after sliding or spinning, then typically began flipping and rolling, spreading chaos with each move.

It is a racing truth that, generally speaking, drivers tend to suffer more significant injuries when their cars hit walls at high speeds than when they lose control and soar through the air, bouncing along the track or apron. Over the years, it has been almost commonplace to watch cars roll and tumble violently only to see drivers step out of the smashed vehicles with no injuries.

That reality, however, didn't blot out the potential danger associated with flying race cars. Officials were concerned not only with driver safety but also the hard reality that flying race cars could cause spectator injuries. The 1993 season had been particularly troublesome. Wild rides were experienced by several drivers. For Rusty Wallace, it was double trouble. His cars went on wild tumbles at Daytona and Talladega, and the violence of those episodes accelerated NASCAR's move toward a solution.

The roof flap was ready by February 1994.

Developed by team owner Jack Roush, members of his engineering group, former driver and crew chief Norman Negre, Cup Series director Gary Nelson and others, the flap was technical but, at its core, simple. Installed on the car roof and hood, the flap is designed to open when the car turns at high speed. The air caught by the flap serves as a brake and as a force to keep the car on the ground.

When they were revealed in 1994, the flaps looked bizarre, but over the years they became an accepted—indeed, a welcomed—part of race cars.

Race cars occasionally still lift into the air but with much less frequency. The flap was a relatively easy fix for a complex issue.

Under the watchful eye of a NASCAR official, crew members work on the roof flaps of the Toyota driven by Michael Waltrip during practice for the NASCAR Sprint Cup Series Coke Zero 400 at Daytona International Speedway on July 4, 2013.

Race fans packed the Darlington Raceway stands as Jeff Gordon took the checkered flag to win the Mountain Dew Southern 500. Gordon won the iconic race four consecutive years from 1995 through 1998.

That last race, with the 1992 championship on the line, ended in remarkable fashion. Alan Kulwicki, a driver who had roared in from Wisconsin to challenge the sport's hierarchy, scored one of NASCAR's biggest upsets by edging Bill Elliott in the race for the championship. Kulwicki, who stubbornly stayed with his own limited-resource team despite being offered rides by bigger teams, scored enough points to edge Elliott by leading the most laps of any driver in the 500. Elliott won the race.

As for Petty, he rolled around in the middle of the field but was caught up in a crash, his Pontiac rolling to a stop inside the track while flames popped from the car. There was momentary fear that Petty could be seriously injured in his final ride, but the danger disappeared quickly and Petty climbed from the car and waved to fans.

Petty's car was hauled to the garage area, and most on the scene assumed the great driver's ride was at an end. But members of the crew jumped into action and repaired the car so that Petty could return to the track and officially take his last checkered flag.

"The team hated not to finish the last lap," Petty said. "They took the front

ABOVE LEFT: **Jeff Gordon takes time to sign autographs along pit road before a Cup Series at Pocono International Raceway in 1995. With his movie star looks and charisma, Gordon was a favorite of almost all NASCAR fans, apart from those who pulled for Dale Earnhardt.**

ABOVE RIGHT: **Brothers Jeff Burton (left) and Ward Burton (right) emerged on the NASCAR Winston Cup scene in the mid-1990s and went on to become one of NASCAR's more successful pairs of racing siblings. The two won a combined twenty-six races, with Jeff Burton recording twenty-one victories and Ward Burton five, including the 2002 Daytona 500.**

of the car off and put a new radiator on. I pulled the car up to the pit area and sat there until the last three or four laps before going back on the track. I didn't want to get in anybody's way."

Finally, it was over.

In the Petty camp, emotions bubbled over in the aftermath of the race. Although Richard Petty's last drive had been planned for more than a year, now reality was rushing in. A journey that had begun decades earlier and had made him internationally famous was over. His wife, Lynda, and daughters Rebecca, Sharon, and Lisa were there for the moment they had both wished for and dreaded for years.

"We went up in the back of the truck, and everybody had a good cry," Richard said. "They were tickled to death we didn't get hurt, tickled to death it was the last race, tickled to death it was over."

In the grandstands, fans waved Petty blue-and-red caps. There were tears there, too, and, he would admit years later, also tears in the eyes of the man who had driven the No. 43 into glory.

Dale Inman, Petty's crew chief, called it "one of the saddest days of my life. I think the girls and Lynda told him to just survive it. Then we got in a wreck. We fixed the car because we wanted him to finish the race. And he did."

The sport would never see his like again.

Two of stock car racing's rising stars would not live to experience NASCAR's grandest successes. Kulwicki, only months after his 1992 championship triumph, died April 1, 1993, along with three associates, when their private plane crashed while attempting to land near Bristol, Tennessee, for that weekend's race. And Davey Allison, son of Bobby Allison and widely regarded as a future champion, died of injuries he suffered in a helicopter crash July 12, 1993, at Talladega Superspeedway. Aviation accidents had robbed the sport of two dedicated competitors who probably would have been dominant forces across the NASCAR landscape for many years to come.

Unfortunately, the decade saw other driver deaths too.

Veteran campaigner J. D. McDuffie died at the age of fifty-two in a race accident at Watkins Glen International in New York. He started 653 races without a win but was a reliable competitor and was widely respected in garage areas. In February 1994, as teams practiced for the Daytona 500, drivers Neil Bonnett and Rodney Orr were killed in separate single-car accidents over a stretch of four days. Orr, thirty-one, died on the same day that Bonnett, forty-seven, was buried in his native Alabama.

Clifford Allison, Bobby Allison's younger son, was killed in August 1992 while practicing at Michigan International Speedway. John Nemechek died from injuries suffered in a Truck Series race at Homestead–Miami Speedway in March 1997. The pickup truck series had made its debut in 1995 as NASCAR's third major national series.

The decade saw a dramatic rebound by driver Ernie Irvan, who suffered life-threatening injuries in a crash at the Michigan track in August 1994. Determined to recover and race again, Irvan worked through fourteen months of healing and rehabilitation and resumed his career. He reached victory lane again in 1996 and, more meaningfully, won at Michigan, the track that almost

The truck series debuted in 1995 as NASCAR's third major national series. The first race in what was then known as the NASCAR Craftsman Truck Series was held at Phoenix International Raceway on February 5, 1995. Mike Skinner, driving the black No. 3 GM Goodwrench Chevy truck, won by .09 seconds over Terry Labonte.

NORTH WILKESBORO SPEEDWAY

Terry Labonte (5) and Elton Sawyer (27) brought the field to the start of the First Union 400 at North Wilkesboro Speedway on April 14, 1996. It was the next-to-last race at the .625-mile track, which was dropped from the NASCAR Cup Series schedule after the 1996 season in favor of larger and more modern facilities. From 1949 to 1996, North Wilkesboro hosted ninety-three Cup Series races.

cost him his life, in 1997. Irvan, winner of the 1991 Daytona 500, retired in 1999 with fifteen Cup victories.

Dale Earnhardt's 1990 Cup championship was scored at the expense of Mark Martin, who lost the title by only twenty-six points. The seasonal result was particularly painful for Martin, who was fined forty-six points two races into the schedule when NASCAR ruled his Roush Fenway Racing Ford carried an illegal carburetor spacer in a win at Richmond. In the broad view, the penalty cost Martin the championship, and it became a bigger loss over the years as he failed to win a title despite being one of the sport's most consistent and dependable racers.

After Earnhardt dominated the first half of the decade in the run for championships, Gordon ruled the second half, winning titles in 1995, 1997, and 1998. Terry Labonte, Gordon's Hendrick Motorsports teammate, won in 1996.

The 1994 season marked the debut of a key safety device—the roof flap. The flaps were positioned on each car's roof and were designed to open when a car turned to the side, thus serving as a brake and, in most cases, preventing cars from flying into the air. Airborne crashes had become a recurring problem.

Harry Gant, who had a long run of success on short tracks before starting his Cup career at the age of thirty-three, won on the big tour for the first time in 1982, aged forty-two. His grandest success came in 1991 when he won four consecutive races—at Darlington, Richmond, Dover, and Martinsville—in September, earning the nickname "Mr. September."

In May 1992, the sport paved the way for big changes in the future as Charlotte Motor Speedway, long one of the most innovative tracks in auto racing, added lights to its facility for that year's Cup All-Star Race. The concept of hosting a superspeedway race at night was revolutionary at the time, but immediate success—Davey Allison won the race despite a last-lap crash with Kyle Petty—led other tracks to follow suit. By 1998, Daytona International Speedway had added lights to the sport's most famous track, and other tracks moved to night racing, primarily to benefit television networks, which preferred later race starts.

On June 7, 1992, Bill France Sr., whose vision for stock car racing had built the foundation for the modern sport, died after a long illness.

As the sport moved toward the future, it left one of its landmark tracks in the past. In 1996 the Cup Series ran its final race at North Wilkesboro (North Carolina) Speedway, which had been a part of the circuit since 1949, its first year. Jeff Gordon was the winner.

In 1999 Dale Jarrett, son of former champion Ned Jarrett, raced to the Cup championship. Seven years earlier, Jarrett signed on to become the first driver for a new team owned by Joe Gibbs, who had coached Washington to three

BELOW LEFT: **NASCAR racing returned to the state of Texas with the completion of Texas Motor Speedway in Fort Worth and the running of its inaugural race on April 6, 1997. Jeff Burton won the 1997 Interstate Batteries 500, marking the first time a Cup Series event had taken a green flag in Texas since the race at the Texas World Speedway in June of 1981.**

BELOW RIGHT: **Ernie Irvan celebrates in Victory Lane after winning the 1996 Jiffy Lube 300 at New Hampshire International Speedway on July 14, 1996. It was the thirteenth of Irvan's 15 career Winston Cup victories, and it came after he had been seriously injured and out of a race car for almost the entire 1995 season. Shown with him is Bill Broderick, who as the Supervisor of Public Relations for Union 76 Racing Division coordinated NASCAR's Victory Lane celebrations for nearly three decades and became known to many fans as simply "The Hat Man."**

After two decades of trying, Dale Earnhardt finally won the Daytona 500. Earnhardt took the checkered flag in the 1998 Daytona 500, which also marked the fortieth running of stock car racing's most prestigious event and kicked off NASCAR's fiftieth-anniversary season.

Super Bowl championships. Gibbs, a fan of fast cars since his teenage years, decided to make racing a family business and steadily built a competitive team. Jarrett gave Gibbs his first Cup win in the Daytona 500 in 1993. Jarrett left the team after three seasons and won the 1999 championship with Robert Yates Racing, one of Ford Motor Company's bedrock teams.

The 1999 season also marked the arrival in the Cup Series of a driver destined to become one of the most famous individuals in NASCAR history. Dale Earnhardt Jr. made his Cup debut in the Coca-Cola 600 at Charlotte after successful seasons in the sport's No. 2 series. Earnhardt Jr. ran the 600 under immense media and fan pressure, his debut sparking the sort of interest rarely seen for a driver competing in his first race. Junior finished sixteenth, ten positions behind his father.

Also in 1999, Mike Helton, who had held several executive positions across the sport, was named NASCAR senior vice president and chief operating officer, thus becoming the first person outside the France family to sit in the big driver's seat controlling the sport. He would remain an important figure in the sport for many years to come.

Growth throughout the 1990s put NASCAR in excellent position to sell its product to television, and officials signed a landmark, multinetwork $2.4–billion deal in 1999, setting up the coming millennium as one of the most anticipated in stock car racing.

After Dale Earnhardt's historic win in the 1998 Daytona 500, pit crew members, NASCAR officials, and others lined pit road to shake Earnhardt's hand in a moving tribute to acknowledge the accomplishment of one of NASCAR's greatest drivers.

Dale Earnhardt raises his hands triumphantly in Victory Lane to celebrate winning the Daytona 500 on his twentieth try. His victory on February 15, 1998, came in the fortieth running of the Great American Race and kicked off a celebration of NASCAR's fiftieth–anniversary season.

ABOVE: **Night racing finally came to the Daytona International Speedway on October 17, 1998, when the Pepsi 400 was run under the lights. The race was originally scheduled for July 4 that year, but out-of-control wildfires throughout Florida forced its postponement. Here Dale Earnhardt leads Rusty Wallace (2) and his Richard Childress Racing teammate Mike Skinner (31) across the stripe in a race eventually won by Jeff Gordon.**

RIGHT: **Jeff Gordon beat Dale Earnhardt to the finish line by .128 seconds to win the 1999 Daytona 500. It was the second of three career Daytona 500 victories for Gordon, who scored his first in 1997 and won again in 2005.**

A SUPERSTAR'S STEPFATHER

John Bickford was the man behind the Man.

Jeff Gordon stormed into NASCAR in 1993 and raced to superstardom and into legend, winning four championships, 93 races, a Hall of Fame election, and changing the face of the sport.

Somebody had to put this winning machine in motion, and that somebody was Bickford, Gordon's stepfather.

Bickford orchestrated Gordon's rise from wonderchild to Superman. He and Gordon's mother, Carol, bought Gordon a quarter-midget racer at the age of 5. The family lived in Vallejo, California, and the Bickfords hauled the car—and Jeff—to a nearby fairgrounds lot. They designed a rough track in the dirt and gravel and turned their son loose.

Soon Gordon had learned enough about the ins and outs of the quarter-midget to move to a real race track. He started racing at Cracker Jack Track (the name later was changed to Roy Hayer Memorial Speedway), a $^1/_{20}$th-mile quarter-midget dirt track in Rio Linda, 50 miles from the Bickford home.

Soon he won. By the age of 7, Gordon was clearly the class of the field at Cracker Jack.

Greg DeCaires raced against Gordon there.

"He and John had a special bond," DeCaires said. "John had him 'debrief' at an early age. As soon as we unbuckled and took the helmets off, we wanted to go play in the dirt. Jeff wasn't allowed to do that. He had to stick with John and hang around the car."

Gordon won on a regular basis. Soon he and the Bickfords moved to bigger and faster tracks, and he kept winning.

Then, when Gordon was 14, Bickford made the decision that changed everything. Because high-level racing opportunities for younger drivers were limited in California, Bickford moved his family to Pittsboro, Indiana, in the middle of sprint and midget racing country.

In Indiana, Gordon's fame spread as he won short-track races against older and more experienced drivers. It was clear he was the way to big things.

His open-wheel experience was leading toward IndyCar racing, but Gordon detoured to NASCAR and became internationally famous as one of the best drivers ever to climb into a stock car.

John Bickford was there at the beginning and for much of the long trip. He advised Gordon along the way as the family enjoyed a journey none of them could have envisioned when Jeff was five.

Jeff Gordon celebrates in Victory Lane with, (from left), his mother, Carol, his stepfather, John, and his wife, Ingrid Vandebosch, after the Gatorade Duel at Daytona International Speedway on February 15, 2007.

RIGHT: **Former Indy Car driver Tony Stewart, the 1991 USAC Rookie of the Year, made the switch to the NASCAR circuit full-time in 1999 with a team owned by Joe Gibbs. Here "Smoke" does an interview in the Daytona International Speedway garage area before his Winston Cup debut in the 1999 Daytona 500.**

BELOW: **The crew of Dale Earnhardt Jr. services his Budweiser Chevy on pit road during his Winston Cup debut in the Coca-Cola 600 at Lowe's Motor Speedway on May 30, 1999. Dale Jr. started eighth that day and came home sixteenth.**

FAR LEFT: **Dale Earnhardt Jr. was practically already a superstar when he made his NASCAR Winston Cup racing debut in the Coca-Cola 600 at Lowe's Motor Speedway in Charlotte, North Carolina, on May 30, 1999. He started eighth that day and finished sixteenth.**

LEFT: **Dale Earnhardt celebrates in Victory Lane after bumping Terry Labonte late in the race to win the 1999 Goody's Headache Powder 500 at Bristol Motor Speedway. The move was virtually a repeat of what Earnhardt had done to "rattle his cage" and beat Labonte in the 1995 Goody's 500. Earnhardt was booed heartily by fans in the stands for one of the few times in his long NASCAR career.**

Bill France Jr., the oldest son of NASCAR founder, Bill France, served as NASCAR's chief executive officer from 1972 until 2000. Mike Helton (middle) became NASCAR vice president and chief operating officer in February 1999, making him the first person outside of the France family to run NASCAR's day-to-day operations.

DALE
EARNHARDT
(1990, 1991, 1993, 1994)

JEFF
GORDON
(1995, 1997, 1998)

CHAMPS

Earnhardt won three Cup championships in the 1980s and remained on course for legendary status in the next decade. He won the title in four of the first five years of the 1990s, with the 1994 championship tying him at that level with the sport's all-time king, Richard Petty. Earnhardt and team owner Richard Childress cemented the perfect partnership over those seasons, and one of racing's best pit crews provided the foundation for Earnhardt's continuing success. His first two titles in the '90s were with crew chief Kirk Shelmerdine. Andy Petree led the RCR team in 1993 and 1994. Shelmerdine and Petree both spoke often of Earnhardt's ability to get the best out of cars that might not be perfect, underlining that as one of the keys to his championship runs.

Gordon changed the NASCAR narrative when he arrived in the sport full-time in 1993. A short-track star who had dazzled in Sprint and Midget cars, he left his planned path to IndyCar racing and settled on NASCAR. He won two races in 1994 and drove to another level in 1995, winning seven times and scoring his first championship. Crew chief Ray Evernham envisioned the Hendrick Motorsports team building a dynasty with Gordon at the center, and that goal was reached as Gordon rang up championships in 1997 (with 10 wins) and 1998 (13 wins). Along the way, Gordon expanded the often-narrow image of a NASCAR racer by appearing on national television shows and traveling with jet-setters. And, not to be overlooked, he won the Daytona 500 twice during the '90s.

ALAN
KULWICKI

(1992)

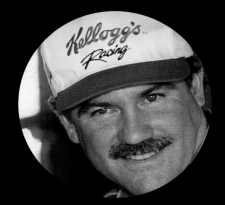

TERRY
LABONTE

(1996)

DALE
JARRETT

(1999)

Kulwicki was NASCAR's ultimate independent. Although he built a strong reputation with some early success, he turned down offers of rides with front-line teams to concentrate on building his own operation. That goal reached its summit at the end of the 1992 season as Kulwicki outran several competitors to win the Cup championship, a remarkable accomplishment for a team considerably smaller in both personnel and financial support than those he passed. At the start of that season, Kulwicki was given little hope of actually challenging for the title, but he famously did things "my way" and hoisted the big trophy at year's end. Sadly Kulwicki's reign as champion was short. In April 1993 he and three colleagues died in the crash of a private plane as they attempted to land near Bristol, Tennessee, for that weekend's race.

In 1978, when businessman Billy Hagan offered Terry Labonte, a short-track winner from Corpus Christi, Texas, a ride in the Cup Series, Labonte quickly accepted, thinking he would be making his Cup debut at North Wilkesboro Speedway or Martinsville Speedway or another short track. Instead Hagan threw Labonte into the fire, putting him in the team's car for the first time at mean ol' Darlington Raceway, a track mastered by very few. Undaunted, Labonte raced fast and smart and finished fourth in his first Cup race, a stunning result on a track as tough as Darlington. That set the course for Labonte's long Cup career. He won his first Cup title in 1984. Many assumed his career was essentially over when he went winless from 1990 to 1993, but he bounced back with Hendrick Motorsports and won his second title in 1996, outrunning teammate Jeff Gordon.

Although Jarrett grew up around racing (his father, Ned, was a two-time Cup champion and managed Hickory Speedway, a North Carolina short track), he wasn't an automatic superstar. He raced mostly full-time in the Cup from 1987 to 1990 without winning. His first checkered flag came in 1991 as he edged Davey Allison for a win at Michigan Speedway. In 1992, Jarrett moved from the Woods Brothers Racing team to a new organization started by long-time National Football League coach Joe Gibbs and won races there before joining Robert Yates Racing. With Yates, Jarrett finally got his Cup title, winning four races, including the Brickyard 400.

Dale Earnhardt (3) and Dale Earnhardt, Jr. (8) race each other during the 2000 Daytona 500. The younger Earnhardt finished thirteenth that day, while his dad posted a twenty-first-place showing. It was one of only two times father and son would get to race each other in the Great American Race.

Chapter 6

THE 2000s

A New and Dark Millennium

By Kelly Crandall

Under caution with six laps to go in the 2000 Winston 500 at Talladega Superspeedway, Dale Earnhardt rode along in seventeenth place. But when the green flag dropped, Earnhardt hooked up with Kenny Wallace and came slicing through the middle of the field in spectacular fashion to win a Winston Millon No Bull bonus and record his tenth Talladega victory and seventy-sixth and final of his career.

NASCAR ENTERED the new millennium riding a wave of growth from the 1990s. But that took a backseat through the first part of the 2000s as the industry was forced to address the ever-growing concern about safety with a rising toll in driver deaths.

Four national series drivers died between May 2000 and February 2001. Fourth-generation driver Adam Petty lost his life in a crash during Busch Series practice at New Hampshire Motor Speedway on May 12, 2000. Petty, who was nineteen years old, hit the Turn 3 wall and suffered a basilar skull fracture.

Kenny Irwin Jr., thirty, crashed in nearly the same spot as Petty at the same track during July practice for the Cup Series race that year. Irwin died from multiple injuries, including to his skull.

In October, Truck Series competitor Tony Roper had a fatal accident at Texas Motor Speedway. Roper, thirty-five, suffered a severe neck injury.

The most significant loss resulted in a faster push toward change. Seven-time champion and NASCAR hero Dale Earnhardt Sr. lost his life after crashing in the final corner of the last lap of the Daytona 500 in 2001. A basilar skull fracture was the cause of death.

Enter the HANS and Hutchens device.

NASCAR mandated that drivers in all three national series wear one of the head-and-neck support devices by October 2001. The devices had been used by a few drivers, but many were not on board with something new that they also considered uncomfortable. By 2005 the HANS was the only device permitted in NASCAR competition.

In a sad twist of fate, Earnhardt had been adamantly against a head-and-neck device.

Next came the SAFER barrier or "soft wall." Having been in development since the 1990s by a team of engineers under Dr. Dean Sicking through the University of Nebraska–Lincoln, the technology allows for a "softer" impact when a car meets the wall. The barrier absorbs the energy, whereas a concrete wall has no give. After it debuted in the 2002 Indianapolis 500, NASCAR required all tracks to install SAFER barriers for the 2003 season.

The evolution of safety continued in waves from tracks to the car and driver safety components. Cockpits now consist of seven-point harness systems. Windshields have gotten stronger. Parts and the pieces on the cars, like roll bars, have changed to protect the drivers. Seats were also moved toward the car's center, and energy-absorbing material was added to door panels.

Many innovations have come from the NASCAR Research and Development Center, a building that opened in Concord, North Carolina, in 2002. No national series driver has died since Earnhardt's accident.

In his final season, Earnhardt gave fans and NASCAR plenty to remember. Early in the season at Atlanta Motor Speedway, Earnhardt edged Bobby Labonte in a photo finish for the victory. But one of the greatest Earnhardt memories came in his final Talladega Superspeedway race in the fall. Earnhardt came from eighteenth to the win in the last few laps for his seventy-sixth and final Winston Cup Series win. While the older Earnhardt would soon be gone, the 2000 season saw the arrival of the son.

BELOW LEFT: **By winning the 2000 Winston Cup Series championship for Joe Gibbs Racing, Bobby Labonte joined his brother Terry as the first siblings to win championships at NASCAR's highest level. Terry Labonte won Cup Series championships in 1984 and 1996.**

BELOW RIGHT: **Car owner Richard Childress enjoys some victory champagne, courtesy of Dale Earnhardt after "the Intimidator" won the 2000 Winston 500 at Talladega Superspeedway in legendary fashion. Riding seventeenth with six laps to go at the 2.66-mile facility, Earnhardt stormed through the field to record his tenth Talladega win and the seventy-sixth and final win of his career. He also collected a $1 million bonus from R. J. Reynolds Tobacco Co. for winning a Winston Million No Bull race.**

Bobby Labonte celebrates his only Winston Cup Series championship with team owner and former Washington Redskins head coach Joe Gibbs (center) and crew chief Jimmy Makar (left) after it became official following the season-ending 2000 NAPA 500 at Atlanta Motor Speedway. Labonte won four races that year, had nineteen top-five finishes, and twenty-four top-ten finishes in thirty-four races, besting runnerup Dale Earnhardt by 265 points.

Dale Earnhardt Jr. moved into the Cup Series alongside friend and friendly rival Matt Kenseth. Earnhardt became the first rookie to win the All-Star Race after qualifying through his first career win at Texas Motor Speedway. Kenseth, meanwhile, won his first race in the Coca-Cola 600 and earned Rookie of the Year honors.

Labonte missed out on the Atlanta win but picked up four victories throughout the season on the way to the championship. Labonte took the honor, his first and only, over Earnhardt.

The 2000 season also marked the end of multiple television networks broad-casting races. A new deal, a unified package, went into effect in 2001 when the season was split between Fox Sports, NBC Sports, and Turner Sports (TNT).

Fox Sports began its tenure with one of the most competitive Daytona 500 races, with forty-nine lead changes. Underdog Michael Waltrip, driving for Earnhardt's team Dale Earnhardt Inc., scored his first career win as his friend and boss disappeared from his rearview mirror. Waltrip had been 0-for-462 in the Cup Series before being hired by Earnhardt.

A week later, Dale Earnhardt Inc. driver Steve Park honored Earnhardt with a win at Rockingham, North Carolina.

Kevin Harvick replaced Earnhardt at Richard Childress Racing. Harvick drove a white and red GM Goodwrench Chevrolet and did so to victory lane at Atlanta Motor Speedway and Chicagoland Speedway.

Then in July, it was NBC Sports at the call for one of the most emotional nights the sport had seen when Earnhardt Jr. returned to Daytona International Speedway and, with teammate Michael Waltrip, his wingman, won the Pepsi 400 in honor of his father.

The first-time-winners club continued with Elliott Sadler at Bristol Motor Speedway. Sadler won his first race in the famed Wood Brothers Racing No. 21 car, which was the first win for the team since 1993.

It was undoubtedly a year of firsts. Dodge returned to NASCAR with Ray Evernham fielding its flagship team. Other Dodge teams included Bill Davis Racing and Felix Sabates.

Sterling Marlin brought Dodge back to victory lane at Michigan International Speedway late in the season. In the season finale, Bill Elliott gave Evernham his first win as a team owner.

The grieving began again as the season made its way into the homestretch. The September 11 terrorist attacks brought racing to a pause, with the series returning to action at Dover International Speedway, where patriotism wasn't hard to find. Cars were adorned in red, white, and blue, while Earnhardt Jr. — quickly becoming the series' most popular driver—pulled off some more magic by winning the race and displaying a giant American flag afterward.

The championship belonged to Jeff Gordon. Gordon went unchallenged and bested Tony Stewart by over 300 points for his fourth and final championship as the season wound down.

NEW FACES CLIMB TO THE TOP OF THE MOUNTAIN

Stewart, of course, didn't stay down long. The 2002 season started with Stewart finishing last in the Daytona 500 due to an engine failure but ending with the Indiana native hoisting his first Winston Cup Series championship.

The path to crowning a new champion was full of drama.

Led by Ray Evernham, former championship-winning crew chief for Jeff Gordon, Dodge made a much-heralded full-time return to the sport in 2001 after being absent since the late 1970s. Dodge supported five teams in its return and put ten entries into the 2001 Daytona 500, including Bill Elliott (right) and Stacy Compton (left) who made up the front row for that year's Great American Race.

Ward Burton took Bill Davis to victory lane in the Daytona 500 after Sterling Marlin was penalized for pulling on his fender under the red flag. Marlin, the leader, climbed out on the backstretch and tugged on his right front fender, which had been damaged after contact with Gordon.

Daytona wouldn't define Marlin's season, however. Marlin and his Chip Ganassi Racing Dodge picked up two wins early in the year at Las Vegas and Darlington and led the point standings for twenty-five of the first twenty-six weeks. It would have been a great story to see Marlin, one of the good ol' boys from Tennessee, win his first championship had unfortunate racing fate not intervened.

A fractured vertebra in his neck sidelined Marlin for the final six races of the year. Injured in a crash at Kanas Speedway, rookie Jamie McMurray took over Marlin's car and pulled off a shocking win in the fall race at Charlotte Motor Speedway—just his second career start.

McMurray was one driver in a wave of young talent to start taking up space in the winner's circle. The likes of Harvick, Kenseth, and Earnhardt Jr.

FUTURISTIC RACE CAR BRINGS TOMORROW, TODAY

With the introduction of a brand-new race car in 2007 came an abbreviation. The Car of Tomorrow—COT—was NASCAR's latest, greatest and, most importantly, safest car.

It was the fifth generation of Cup Series car and a departure from what the sport had previously competed. Not only was the COT noticeably boxier, but it was odd when compared to its predecessors. Why? Firstly it featured a front splitter under the grille with metal braces that weren't the strongest when made contact with.

Second it had a rear wing. Yes, a wing.

The COT was also symmetrical and all bodies, regardless of the manufacturer nameplate, basically looked the same. NASCAR officials also hoped it would be a cost-save for teams as a vehicle that could compete on different racetracks instead of building track-specific cars.

But the car had many safety advances after years of development. Among those innovations were stronger A-frames and additional roll bars in the cockpit. Speaking of the cockpit, it was roomier for the driver as the seat was positioned more toward the center of the car. An energy-absorbing foam was also installed between the roll cage and the door panel.

"It's about time," Richard Petty said. "We've been running basically the same car since 1981, and all they've done is refine it. The big deal is safety. You're never going to make it one hundred percent safe, but you put safety in it, and then you just throw the car around it."

In 2007 the COT debuted in sixteen races before being rolled out full-time in 2008. Kyle Busch won its first race on March 25 at Bristol Motor Speedway. In victory lane, Busch then gave a memorable review.

"I'm still not a fan of these things," Busch said. "I can't stand to drive them—they suck."

However, for as much as the COT was a talking point because of how it raced or looked, there was no denying it did the job it was built to do. Two breathtaking accidents in its first two full seasons saw both drivers walk away without a scratch.

The first was April 4, 2008, when Michael McDowell walked away from a terrifying qualifying crash at Texas Motor Speedway. McDowell's car got loose going into Turn 1 and shot up the track head-first into the outside SAFER barrier. The contact sent the car airborne and onto its roof, sliding along the track before beginning a series of barrel rolls. Fortunately the car came to a stop on all four wheels.

On April 26, 2009, Carl Edwards was sent airborne into the catch fence at Talladega superspeedway. Edwards tried to block Brad Keselowski on the last lap, and contact sent him on the track, and when his car was hit by Ryan Newman into the air, the car was ripped apart, but Edwards climbed out unhurt. Unfortunately, seven fans were injured from the flying debris, but they were all non-life-threatening.

NASCAR ran the COT from 2007 to 2012.

U.S. Transportation Secretary Norman Y. Mineta (right), discusses SAFER barriers with inventor and engineer Dr. Dean Sicking on May 15, 2004, at Richmond International Raceway.

continued to earn wins while newcomers Ryan Newman and Jimmie Johnson looked like anything but rookies. Newman and Johnson combined for four wins, and Johnson even led the point standings for one week after the fall Kansas Speedway race.

Kurt Busch burst into stardom with his first win at Bristol Motor Speedway driving for Jack Roush. Busch then kept winning for four by the end of the season.

WINSTON WAVES THE WHITE FLAG

NASCAR was in a good spot going into 2003, with a mix of young and experienced talent fighting duking it out each week. And it was a young driver who took the series by storm that season.

Kenseth earned his first and only win in the third race of the year at Las Vegas Motor Speedway. From there, Kenseth might not have won again, and yet he was untouchable through remarkable consistency that built the No. 17 Roush Fenway Raciing an insurmountable point lead.

Taking the championship point lead after the fourth race of the season, Kenseth clinched the title with one week to spare at Rockingham Speedway. Up over 200 points on Johnson, it was enough to give Kenseth and team owner Jack Roush their first championships, respectively, in the Winston Cup Series.

"It's kind of like going through a plate-glass window," said Roush, who had finished second in the championship with driver Mark Martin four times in the 1990s. "There's a lot of pain breaking through it."

A duel between Ricky Craven and Busch wrote a new page in the history books in 2003. Craven edged Busch in the spring race at Darlington Raceway after the two traded the lead and traded paint multiple times over the final few laps. Craven was the winner at the finish line by 0.002 seconds in the closest

Dale Earnhardt holds court with Tony Stewart (left), Dale Earnhardt Jr., and Rusty Wallace (right) before the start of the 2001 Daytona 500. It would be the last race of Earnhardt's legendary NASCAR career, which spanned twenty-seven years and 676 Cup Series races.

finish in Cup Series history at the time. It was a record that would stand until it was tied at Talladega Superspeedway in 2011.

Darlington was Craven's final win in the series. It was also the last win for Pontiac in NASCAR as they left the sport at the end of the year.

Competitor safety came back to the forefront of conversation in September 2003. When Dale Jarrett was involved in a crash at New Hampshire that left his car sitting in the middle of the frontstretch as the field raced back to the caution, it was clear a change was needed. It resulted in NASCAR officials deciding to freeze the field when the caution came out, and awarding a "free pass" to the first driver one lap down.

As the year drew to a close, NASCAR prepared to bid goodbye to one of its most recognizable partners. R. J. Reynolds had announced in February it was looking to leave the sport, which indeed came to fruition.

Winston had been a staple in NASCAR since becoming the entitlement sponsor of the premier series in 1971, but the times had changed, and the company decided to end its sponsorship program.

Dale Earnhardt raced competitively throughout the 2001 Daytona 500, running third behind Michael Waltrip and Dale Earnhardt Jr. coming through Turn 4 on the final lap, just prior to the crash that would claim his life.

Michael Waltrip celebrates after winning the 2001 Daytona 500 while driving for Dale Earnhardt Inc. Waltrip would soon receive word that his boss and close friend had been critically injured in a wreck in Turn 4 on the final lap. It was Waltrip's first career victory and came in his 463rd Cup Series start.

Steve Park pays tribute to his late boss, Dale Earnhardt, in Victory Lane after winning the 2001 Dura Lube 400 at North Carolina Speedway in Rockingham, North Carolina. The race was the next one on the schedule following Earnhardt's fatal crash. Park recorded the second and final victory of his Cup Series career.

CHASING A CHAMPIONSHIP

And so the door opened for NASCAR to make a radical change both in its branding and its championship. In 2004 the premier series became the Nextel Cup Series, featuring a playoff format dubbed the Chase for the Championship. Over the final ten races of the year, ten drivers were eligible after having their points reset in increments of five.

Earnhardt Jr. became a championship contender on the strength of his best season yet, with four wins in the first twenty-six races. Daytona was first. The Earnhardt family legacy continued with Earnhardt Jr. becoming a Daytona 500 winner for the first time in his fourth attempt.

In the season's second race, Kenseth edged rising star Kasey Kahne in a photo finish at Rockingham Speedway. Kenseth's margin of victory was 0.010 seconds.

A victory for Gordon at Talladega Superspeedway in April wasn't met with the same enthusiasm. Gordon was pelted with beer cans after being declared the winner over Earnhardt Jr. when the caution came out on lap 185 of 188.

The inaugural edition of the Chase featured a who's who of drivers. Earnhardt Jr., Gordon, and Johnson were in the mix, as were defending champion Kenseth, Elliott Sadler, and Ryan Newman. Underdog Jeremy Mayfield and his Ray Evernham team made a dramatic entrance into the mix by winning the final race of the regular season.

Busch, Kenseth, and Earnhardt Jr. were the top three in the first race of the Chase. Busch threw the early punch toward his championship foes.

Midway through the Chase for the Championship, Busch led the standings over Earnhardt Jr. by twenty-four points. But Johnson was charging, having won two straight races at Charlotte Motor Speedway and Martinsville Speedway.

But there was no celebrating Johnson's sixth win of the season. After the checkered flag flew at Martinsville, Johnson, and the rest of his Hendrick Motorsports teammates were informed that a team plane had crashed in mountainous terrain in Virginia en route to the race, killing all on board.

Rick Hendrick lost his son Ricky, brother John, nieces Kimberley and Jennifer, and team engine builder Randy Dorton. Others on board were Joe Jackson, Jeff Turner, Scott Lathum, and pilots Dick Tracy and Liz Morrison.

For the remainder of the season, Hendrick teams ran a memorial sticker on the hood of their Chevrolets instead of a sponsor logo. Johnson pulled off an emotional victory a week after the tragedy by winning the race at Atlanta Motor Speedway.

"Once I got in the car today and knew what I was supposed to do, I honestly forgot about everything until I took the checkered flag," said Johnson. "It doesn't change anything, and we don't get back our friends that we lost. But it sure makes all of us feel a little better to be able to do something like this."

Johnson and Gordon couldn't bring the championship back to Hendrick Motorsports, but it wasn't without trying. In a drama-filled finale that saw Busch lose a right-front tire while coming to pit road, bringing out a timely caution, Busch finished fifth and won his first championship. Johnson, who finished second in the race, finished second in the championship by eight points. Gordon finished third in the race and third in the championship by sixteen points.

Jack Roush suddenly had two championships sitting on his mantel.

The 2001 Dura Lube 400 was run on Monday, February 26, 2001, having been postponed the previous day by bad weather. Dale Earnhardt Inc. driver Steve Park started on the front row alongside pole winner Jeff Gordon and went on to win the race. The win came at North Carolina Speedway in Rockingham, North Carolina, and was the second and final victory of Park's Cup Series career.

In just his third start for Richard Childress, racing in the car that belonged to Dale Earnhardt, rookie Kevin Harvick nips Jeff Gordon at the stripe, winning the 2001 Cracker Barrel Old Country Store 500 at Atlanta Motor Speedway. Harvick's memorable first Cup Series win came just three weeks after Dale Earnhardt was killed in a last-lap crash in the 2001 Daytona 500. The official margin of victory was .006 seconds, making it one of the closest finishes in NASCAR history.

Kevin Harvick celebrates after winning the 2001 Cracker Barrel Old Country Store 500 at Atlanta Motor Speedway in storybook fashion. Making just his third start for Richard Childress Racing in the ride that was previously driven by Dale Earnhardt, Harvick beat Jeff Gordon to the stripe by .006 seconds, making it one of the closest finishes in NASCAR history.

TWICE AS NICE FOR STEWART

Stewart added a second championship to his collection in 2005. Of his eventual five race wins during his championship-winning season, Stewart finally conquered his beloved Indianapolis Motor Speedway for his first triumph at the Brickyard and his home track. Stewart was the dominant driver in 2005 through both the regular season and the postseason. He led 1,845 laps and had just one DNF (did not finish) in thirty-six races.

While Stewart was further solidifying his Hall of Fame résumé, a new star broke onto the scene. And it was fitting such a star was in Rick Hendrick's stable. Kyle Busch easily won Rookie of the Year honors and two races.

Busch's first career win at Auto Club Speedway in September made him the youngest winner in Cup Series history at twenty years, four months, and two days. A record that stood until 2009, when Joey Logano broke it at nineteen years, one month, four days.

THE JIMMIE JOHNSON ERA

As the decade continued, NASCAR saw more drivers come into their own. In 2006 it was Johnson—and in 2007, 2008, 2009, and 2010.

Johnson and the No. 48 team led by Chad Knaus became an unreal tear through the Cup Series in 2006 by claiming their first championship. That same season, Johnson won his first Daytona 500 and Brickyard 400.

Dale Earnhardt Jr. (right) and his Dale Earnhardt Inc. teammate Michael Waltrip share a poignant moment after Dale Jr. won the 2001 Pepsi 400 at Daytona International Speedway on July 7, 2001. The win came nearly five months after his father, Dale Earnhardt Sr., passed away due to injuries suffered during the final lap of the 2001 Daytona 500.

TRAGEDY RESULTS IN SAFETY ADVANCES

The loss of Dale Earnhardt in the final corner of the last lap of the 2001 Daytona 500 at Daytona International Speedway rocked NASCAR and its community.

The day had been shaping up to have a storybook ending with Earnhardt's driver Michael Waltrip heading toward his first career win in the season's biggest race. Behind Waltrip was Earnhardt's son, Dale Earnhardt Jr.

Instead it turned into one of the sport's darkest days.

Earnhardt was stock car racing's Superman and it seemed impossible to lose him in a race car, let alone at a racetrack he loved. Fans related to Earnhardt for his rags-to-riches story, entertaining antics, the time he gave to those in need or who simply wanted to meet him, and of course, the Intimidator persona.

On the other hand, NASCAR had in Earnhardt a leader in the garage with a voice that mattered when he used it on topics big and small. Earnhardt was never shy about walking into the official's hauler to grab the ear of Bill France Sr. and Bill France Jr.

Earnhardt was NASCAR, and his loss left a void. Gone was a popular driver and respected competitor. Even more so, with the loss of Earnhardt came the stark realization that NASCAR officials needed to do more about safety and do it fast.

"His presence transcended outside of just NASCAR," said NASCAR chief operating officer Steve O'Donnell. "The sport was really growing, and maybe some of the ideas (about safety) outside of the garage bubble came from (his death) as well because of how big a star he was and how big a name he was."

Earnhardt's legacy is in the HANS device, which NASCAR made a requirement by October 2001. Other safety modifications came in the following years with safer parts and pieces on the cars and then a brand-new car in the Car of Tomorrow (COT). There was also the implementation of SAFER barriers, which were first installed at Indianapolis Motor Speedway.

Earnhardt died of a basilar skull fracture, resulting in a what-if question about the innovations being around before his crash: What difference could the HANS device have made if Earnhardt had no choice but to wear one?

In the wake of his death, widow Teresa Earnhardt and the Earnhardt family fought to keep his autopsy results private. Later that year, Florida passed the Earnhardt Family Protection Act that made autopsy photos, video and audio recordings confidential.

A kid from Kannapolis, North Carolina, Earnhardt followed in his father Ralph's footsteps by becoming a driver. Earnhardt raced hard from the very beginning because prize money meant food on the table.

A seven-time NASCAR champion, Earnhardt won races all across the country on all types of racetracks. Seventy-six races, in fact. None bigger, however, than the 1998 Daytona 500, which was a race that took him twenty years to win.

Earnhardt was awarded the Most Popular Driver Award posthumously in 2001.

Jeff Gordon (24) makes a last-lap pass on teammate Jimmie Johnson en route to his sixth victory of the season in the 2007 UAW-Ford 500. It was the first Car of Tomorrow test race prior to the full launch.

For Johnson and Knaus, the success came after Hendrick had to sit the two down before the season started in what is now known as the "milk and cookies" meeting. Coming off a bitter defeat in the 2005 title chase, Johnson and Knaus were bickering so much that Hendrick sat the two down with milk, cookies, and Mickey Mouse paper plates to emphasize how they were behaving like children.

It was just what the two needed. Johnson and Knaus went on to win five straight championships from 2006 to 2010 and, in the process, set a record. No driver had ever won more than three consecutive titles.

In those five years, Johnson won thirty-five races.

Ten of them came in the 2007 season, in which Johnson got the best of his mentor, Gordon. The series saw Johnson and Gordon trade wins often, with Johnson pulling ahead in the championship fight in the final weeks when he won four straight races at Martinsville, Atlanta, Texas, and Phoenix.

Johnson's ten wins trumped Gordon's incredible thirty top-ten finishes. In the end, his championship margin was seventy-seven points over Gordon.

But Gordon did earn one big celebratory moment during the season. In April, a win at Phoenix Raceway tied Gordon with the late Dale Earnhardt on the all-time wins list, at seventy-six. Gordon recognized his friend and rival by carrying a No. 3 flag around on his victory lap.

"It means the world," Gordon said. "Holding that three flag, it's certainly by no means saying we're as good as him. I learned so much from him. We wanted to honor him. We've been holding onto that flag for a long time."

Like the rest of the sports world, NASCAR postponed its upcoming event in the wake of the terrorist attacks on the United States on September 11, 2001. When racing returned September 23, 2001, at Dover Downs International Speedway, Dale Earnhardt Jr. won the MBNA Cal Ripken Jr. 400 and proudly displayed Old Glory as part of his postrace celebration.

Ward Burton (No. 22) won the 2002 Daytona 500 in a surprising fashion after a momentary lapse in judgment by Sterling Marlin (No. 40) late in the race put the strongest car at the rear of the field. After a wreck brought out a caution on Lap 196, NASCAR red flagged the field so the race could finish under green, and Marlin climbed from his car and tugged at his right front fender. NASCAR considered that as working on the car during a red-flag period, which is illegal, and penalized Marlin for the infraction. When the race restarted, Burton held on for three laps to record the most memorable of his five career Cup Series victories.

Gordon's victory came while driving the Car of Tomorrow, the next generation of race car NASCAR was getting ready to switch to full-time in 2008. It was a safer, boxier race car that was used in sixteen races in 2007.

The car debuted in March 2007 when Kyle Busch drove it to victory lane at Bristol Motor Speedway. And yet, despite being the race winner, Busch proclaimed on television, "I'm still not a big fan of these things. I can't stand to drive them—they suck."

Phoenix, where Gordon won, was the car's second race.

NASCAR didn't just welcome a new car in 2007 but also a new manufacturer. Toyota became the first Japanese manufacturer to field entries at the sport's highest level, which was met with resistance from fans. Reception for a foreign manufacturer was not kind, and it didn't help that their first race, the Daytona 500, involved a cheating scandal.

Michael Waltrip Racing was found to have a mysterious, illegal substance in its fuel that resulted in a 100-point loss and the immediate suspension of Waltrip's crew chief David Hyder, who was also fined $100,000, and director of competition Bobby Kennedy.

It was the start of plenty of growing pains for Toyota. Its teams—MWR, Bill Davis Racing, and Team Red Bull—not only struggled to find success but sometimes missed qualifying for races entirely.

But a rough rookie season gave way to bigger things in 2008 when Joe Gibbs Racing was brought into the fold. More on that in a moment.

The 2008 season was also the Car of Tomorrow's Daytona 500 debut, and the Cup Series was rebranded the Sprint Cup Series with the merger of Nextel and Sprint. For the biggest race of the year, celebrating its fiftieth anniversary, the Harley J. Earl Trophy that is awarded to the winner was plated in gold instead of silver.

Ryan Newman and Roger Penske took home that trophy after the race came down to a three-lap duel. Tony Stewart led the way, but Newman had team-mate Kurt Busch committed to his back bumper and a push down the back-stretch on the final lap to power around the outside of Stewart, who went low in front of Kyle Busch.

Newman's Dodge was clear of the field by Turn 3. The rest is history. Newman and Penske were the victors (the first for both in the event) as Stewart again had the chance for his first win spoiled.

BELOW: **Ward Burton (22) celebrates in Victory Lane after winning the 2002 Daytona 500 in a bizarre fashion.**

Subbing for an injured Sterling Marlin, Jamie McMurray set a NASCAR modern era record when he won the 2002 UAW-GM Quality 500 at Lowe's Motor Speedway in just his second career Cup Series start. McMurray led a race-high of ninety-six laps to drive to Victory Lane that day in Charlotte. McMurray's mark still stands, but it was later tied by Trevor Bayne, who won the 2011 Daytona 500 in just his second career Cup Series start as well.

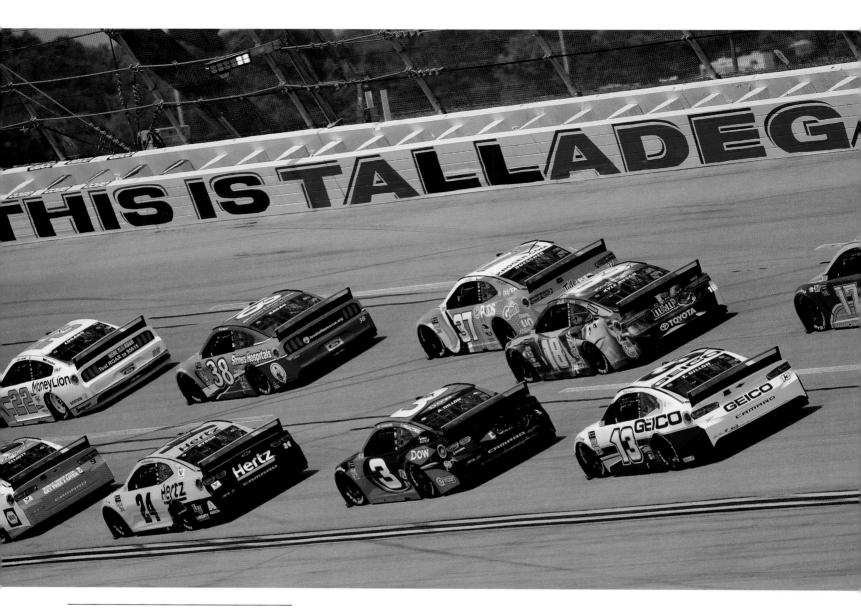

The Steel and Foam Energy Reduction Barrier (known as SAFER Barrier) was developed by Dr. Dean Sicking and a team of engineers at the Midwest Roadside Safety Facility at the University of Nebraska in Lincoln, Nebraska, in the late 1990s and early 2000s. Its first permanent installation at a racetrack came in May 2002, at the Indianapolis Motor Speedway. Shown here at the top of this photo from Talladega Superspeedway, it is now an integral component of the safety measures in place at all NASCAR-sanctioned tracks.

Ford won the season's second and third races with Carl Edwards. Then it was Toyota's turn. Kyle Busch, also new to Joe Gibbs Racing after being let go by Rick Hendrick when Earnhardt Jr. signed with the organization, gave Toyota its first win in the Cup Series at Atlanta Motor Speedway, with teammate Tony Stewart coming home second in a Gibbs/Toyota 1–2 finish.

"Kyle has been very close since the beginning of the year," said Jim Aust, then president of Toyota Racing Development. "Starting with the Daytona 500 and what could have been. To have Kyle come in and take this one and Tony finish second, wow! The feeling can't get any better than that. Finishing one–two for our first Cup win—I don't know how you improve on that."

Kurt Busch (left) and Ricky Craven (right) race off to the finish of the 2003 Carolina Dodge Dealers 400 on March 16 at Darlington Raceway. The two traded paint all the way around the 1.36-mile Darlington Raceway during the final lap, with Craven taking a .002-second victory in what is still considered the closest finish in NASCAR history.

NASCAR's original "Iron Man," Terry Labonte, races Hendrick Motorsports teammate Joe Nemechek en route to his final career victory in the 2003 Mountain Dew Southern 500 at Darlington Raceway. It was Labonte's second Southern 500 win and came almost twenty-three years to the day after he won his first race. Labonte first went to Darlington's Victory Lane on September 1, 1980, and his last trip came on August 31, 2003.

Earnhardt leaving the family-owned team was one of the biggest shocks in the sport's history. It all came to a head when Earnhardt and stepmother Teresa Earnhardt could not agree on how the business should be run and when Earnhardt was denied the 51 percent ownership stake that he sought.

"After intensive efforts to extend my contract at DEI, it's time to move on and drive for another team," Earnhardt said. "We worked hard, but it became evident it just wasn't in the cards. I've done other contracts there, but this one was ten times as hard, ten times the effort. In the end, we never came close. We both want to be at the same place, it just was a difference of opinion on how we were going to get there."

Rusty Wallace takes the checkered flag for the final time in his Hall of Fame Cup Series career to win the 2004 Advance Auto Parts 500 at Martinsville Speedway. Wallace won seven times at the .526-mile paperclip of a track, including a stretch of five wins out of the seven races run in the mid-1990s. It was the fifty-fifth victory of his Cup Series career.

Finding a new home didn't take long, and Earnhardt discovered another father figure in Rick Hendrick. Earnhardt won his first race with his new Hendrick Motorsports No. 88 team at Michigan International Speedway. The victory broke a seventy-eight-race winless drought for Earnhardt.

It was the only win Earnhardt had with his new team. Busch, meanwhile, won eight races with his group at Gibbs, the most he's won in a single season. But after going into the postseason as the point leader, Busch finished fifteenth or worse in the first four races to take him out of championship contention early.

Johnson joined Cale Yarborough as the only driver to win three consecutive Cup Series championships with a fifteenth-place finish. It was all that was needed to earn the title by sixty-nine points over Carl Edwards, who won the season finale at Homestead-Miami Speedway for his ninth victory of the season.

Yarborough made a surprise visit to the season-end awards banquet in New York to present Johnson with the champion's ring. And Yarborough couldn't help but remind Johnson that he only shared a piece of the record.

"You know, all he really did is tie the record—he still has to break it," Yarborough joked on stage. "He still has some work to do."

FROM PITTSBURGH TO PIT ROAD

Chip Ganassi might have entered NASCAR by buying control of an already existing race team, the famed SABCO group, but once he was a team owner, Ganassi found success his way.

Chip Ganassi Racing with Felix Sabates hit the track in 2001 and would go on to employ some of the biggest names in racing. It started with young star Jason Leffler teaming alongside veteran Sterling Marlin.

Two victories in 2001 and a third-place finish in the championship standings for Marlin looked to be the start of something great. And while Ganassi would certainly rack up plenty of accomplishments in the 20-plus years he fielded cars, winning a Cup Series championship wasn't one of them.

Although the big trophy looked to be theirs for the taking in 2002. Marlin put on an impressive campaign with two wins through the first half of the year and led the point standing for 25 of the first 26 weeks. But an accident in the 29th race of the season at Kansas Speedway fractured vertebrae in Marlin's neck, taking him out of the car.

Ganassi went to upstart Jamie McMurray to fill Marlin's seat. In a fairytale story, McMurray won in his second start at Charlotte Motor Speedway. McMurray was promoted to a Cup ride full-time the following year, winning Rookie of the Year honors.

It was a fruitful pairing for both. So much so, that McMurray drove for Ganassi twice in his career.

Together Ganassi and McMurray won the Daytona 500 and Indianapolis in the same season (2010).

Over time the look of the team might have changed—there was the merger with Teresa Earnhardt in 2009 that lasted only a few seasons, and the many talent acquisitions like Juan Pablo Montoya, Kyle Larson, Kurt Busch, and Ross Chastain—but the passion and push for success never waned.

Ganassi's teams won from Daytona to Michigan and on superspeedways to short tracks. There were two All-Star Race wins with $1 million paydays.

Along the way, Ganassi, a former racer from Pittsburgh, became one of the most respected car owners in the garage.

Before all was said and done, before Ganassi, who was not thinking about exiting the sport was suddenly given an offer he couldn't refuse from Justin Marks, his teams won 20 races and 36 poles.

Driver Juan Pablo Montoya, (left), shares a laugh with car owner Chip Ganassi, (right), before the start of the qualifying race for the Daytona 500 on February 11, 2007.

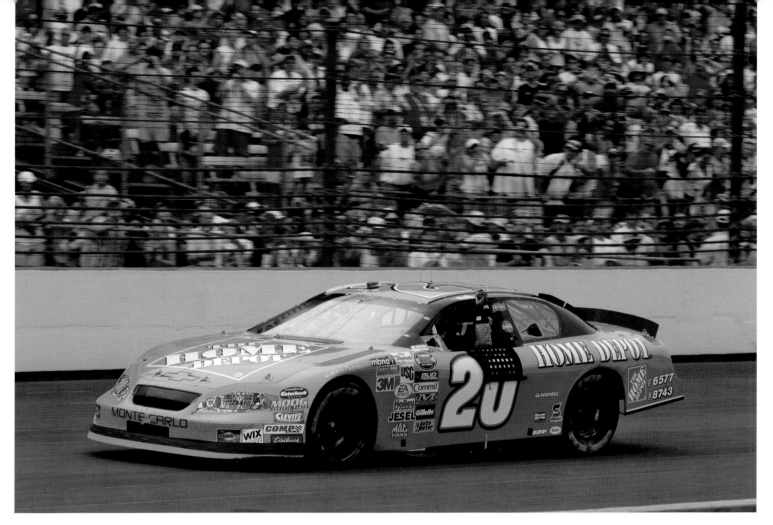

ABOVE: **Tony Stewart waves to part of an estimated crowd of 280,000 on his parade lap after winning the 2005 Brickyard 400 at Indianapolis Motor Speedway. It took the Columbus, Indiana, native twelve tries before he finally claimed the bucket-list victory on August 7, 2005, en route to winning his first Cup Series championship for Joe Gibbs Racing. He won the race again in 2007.**

RIGHT: **Tony Stewart and some of his acquaintances go through the ritual of kissing the bricks at the Brickyard after Stewart won the Brickyard 400 for the first time on August 7, 2005. Dale Jarrett began the practice after winning the third Brickyard in 1996, and it is now considered to be one of the NASCAR Cup Series' most time-honored traditions.**

Johnson took care of that in the final year of the decade, when he indeed broke the record. Johnson won his fourth title by a whopping 141 points over new Hendrick Motorsports teammate Mark Martin. In a career resurgence driving the No. 5 Chevrolet, Martin won five races in his first full season in three years.

Hendrick Motorsports swept the top three spots in points as Gordon finished behind Johnson and Martin. Hendrick drivers combined for thirteen wins, but none of them came from Earnhardt Jr. He struggled in 2009, missing the play-offs, going winless, and finishing twenty-fifth in the standings.

As the Hendrick powerhouse rolled on, a new team debuted. Stewart departed Joe Gibbs Racing and partnered with Gene Haas to form the Chevrolet team Stewart–Haas Racing. Stewart was both driver and co-owner and also brought in Ryan Newman for the organization's second car.

Kyle Busch entered the Cup Series to much fanfare at age nineteen in 2004, but it took him thirty-one races before he visited Victory Lane for the first time. Driving for Hendrick Motorsports, Busch led ninety-five laps and overcame a green–white–checker finish to take the 2005 Sony HD 500 at California Speedway in Fontana, California, on September 4, 2005. Busch went on to win a second race that season and earn Rookie of the Year honors.

ABOVE: **Jimmie Johnson dominated the NASCAR Cup Series in the 2000s, winning thirty-five races and an incredible five championships from 2006 to 2010. Johnson went on to win Cup Series championships in 2013 and 2016, totaling seven throughout his career and tying him with Richard Petty and Dale Earnhardt for the most Cup Series Championship wins in NASCAR history.**

RIGHT: **Chad Knaus served as crew chief for Jimmie Johnson and the No. 48 Lowe's Chevy for all seven of Johnson's championship-winning seasons. He is regarded by many as one of the brightest, most innovative technical minds ever to set foot in the NASCAR Cup Series garage.**

Stewart won four races in the team's first year. But you always remember the first, which came in the June race at Pocono Raceway in Stewart's case.

"I've always had a great group of people to work with at Gibbs, but it's just a little different when it's your own, you know, when you're the one that's got to be accountable for it," Stewart said.

And so, as NASCAR got set to begin its next chapter, many wondered how much more Stewart could accomplish and, most importantly, could Johnson be stopped?

From 2001 to 2006, Dale Jarrett sported the UPS colors on the No. 88 Ford of Yates Racing, and he delivered the sponsor eight victories in that span. He finished his NASCAR Cup Series career with Michael Waltrip Racing, running twenty-nine races across 2007 and 2008 in the No. 44 with the UPS colors aboard, including five races in 2008 that served as his farewell tour.

BOBBY LABONTE
(2000)

JEFF GORDON
(2001)

TONY STEWART
(2002, 2005)

CHAMPS

Bobby Labonte, the younger brother of two-time champion Terry, joined the club with his first and only championship in 2000. It was also the first for team owner Joe Gibbs. Consistency earned Labonte the title as his average finish over thirty-four races was 7.4, with four wins and twenty-four top-ten finishes. Among those wins were two Crown Jewel events: Indianapolis and the Southern 500 at Darlington.

Once the kid who couldn't be stopped, Gordon's final championship was in 2001. Gordon led the series in every statistical category along the way: six wins, twenty-four top-ten finishes, six poles, 2,320 laps led, and an average finish of 9.5. Two consecutive wins in the summer at Dover and Michigan gave Gordon the point lead for the final time, and he easily went on to win the championship by over 300 points.

When the 2002 season opened, Stewart was last in points because of a blown engine. He ended the year first with his first championship. Stewart didn't take the point lead until after the thirtieth race of the season, Talladega, when he finished second. And his final margin over second place in the point standings, Mark Martin, was a slim thirty-eight points after winning three races. Stewart's second championship came on the strength of five wins on the season, including a first for him in the summer Daytona and at his beloved Indianapolis Motor Speedway. However, the most impressive part was that Stewart didn't win a race in the Chase but used consistency to climb to the top with seven top-ten finishes in the final ten races.

MATT KENSETH

(2003)

KURT BUSCH

(2004)

JIMMIE JOHNSON

(2006, 2007, 2008, 2009)

Incredible consistency netted Kenseth his first championship and led to a change in the championship structure. The quiet and mild-mannered Kenseth won just one race in the third week of the season at Las Vegas, and from there was a squatter in the upper half of the result sheet week in and week out. Kenseth earned twenty-five top-ten finishes in thirty-six races.

Busch was the driver who came out on top in the debut season of the Chase for the Championship. After Busch won the opening race of the Chase in New Hampshire to give him a season sweep at the racetrack, he finished outside the top ten just once over the next nine races and a fifth-place finish in the finale at Homestead-Miami Speedway earned him the championship.

The student of Gordon became the teacher when Johnson took over the series with a string of championships never seen before. In '06 Johnson won the Daytona 500 and at Indianapolis, becoming just the second driver to win those races in the same year. In '07 Johnson won ten races in a back-and-forth fight with Gordon in the Chase. But when Johnson won four straight races from late October to mid-November, it turned the championship tide in his favor for good.

A record-tying third straight title in '08 came with a second win at Indianapolis. Johnson led the point standings for nine of the final ten weeks in the Chase, and a victory in the penultimate race at Phoenix Raceway gave Johnson a healthy gap to protect in the finale, which he did.

Championship number four came after winning seven races during the '09 season. Johnson won 28 races across his four championship seasons.

Kyle Busch became the first driver in history to sweep a racing weekend by winning all three races in NASCAR's top three divisions when he prevailed at Bristol Motor Speedway in August 2010. Busch won the Camping World Truck Series run on Wednesday night and the Nationwide Series race run on Friday night. He started nineteenth and led 283 of 500 laps to win the Sprint Cup Irwin Tools Night Race on Saturday.

Chapter 7

THE
2010s

Quintessential NASCAR

By Kelly Crandall

Trevor Bayne was the surprise winner of the 2011 Daytona 500, driving the famed No. 21 Wood Brothers' Ford. It was the only victory of Bayne's career in 187 starts at the Cup Series level.

STANDARDIZED START TIMES. Three attempts at a green-and-white-checkered finish. Have at it, boys. Those were the three storylines as NASCAR began a new decade.

Fans' feedback led to start times of either 1 p.m., 3 p.m., or 7:30 p.m. on the East Coast.

Other changes were set to be implemented on the racetrack. As the Car of Tomorrow continued to go through changes, NASCAR officials informed teams that in the spring of 2010, the wing would be removed for a more traditional blade spoiler. The change kicked into effect at Martinsville Speedway in March.

But before cars ever got on track in 2010, NASCAR vice president Robin Pemberton used the now memorable phrase, "Have at it, boys," to signal drivers would have more leeway to settle their disputes. Something Jeff Gordon and Jeff Burton put to good use at Texas Motor Speedway. Unhappy with contact that left them both wrecked, Gordon marched over to Burton on the backstretch, shoved him, and the scuffle was on.

ABOVE: **The NASCAR Hall of Fame became a reality when it officially opened its doors in Charlotte, North Carolina, on May 11, 2010. The Hall of Fame, which covers a 150,000-square-foot area in downtown Charlotte and includes a nineteen-story office building as part of the complex, cost $160 million to construct.**

LEFT: **One of the most prominent features of the NASCAR Hall of Fame is Glory Road, a 33-degree banked ramp (matching that in the famed Talladega Superspeedway turns) that can feature up to eighteen different cars. It is also used to salute past and current tracks on the NASCAR circuit.**

Team owner Roger Penske joyously sprays his driver Brad Keselowski with champagne as they celebrate with their crew in Victory Lane following Keselowski's victory at the 2012 Geico 400 at Chicagoland Speedway. Keselowski won five races that season en route to his first Cup Series championship, which was also Penske's first NASCAR championship as well during his four decades in the sport.

In a head-on crash into a concrete wall not covered by a SAFER barrier during the 2015 season-opening Xfinity Series race at Daytona International Speedway, Kyle Busch suffered a compound fracture of his right leg and a left mid-foot fracture. Busch missed eleven races that season, but came back to win five Cup Series races and qualified for the playoffs, where he went on to win the title for the first time in his career.

During that same race, Chad Knaus made the unprecedented move of benching his struggling No. 48 Hendrick Motorsports pit crew for Gordon's No. 24 crew. The move helped keep Jimmie Johnson in championship contention, as he was just weeks away from claiming yet another—his fifth.

Action and attitude weren't hard to find around the garage. Brad Keselowski and Carl Edwards tangled at Atlanta Motor Speedway. Edwards returned to the race, and his retaliation sent Keselowski's car airborne into the wall.

Kyle Busch took on NASCAR, also at Texas. Busch was unhappy with a speeding penalty and made an obscene gesture at officials while being held on pit road. It cost Busch two more laps.

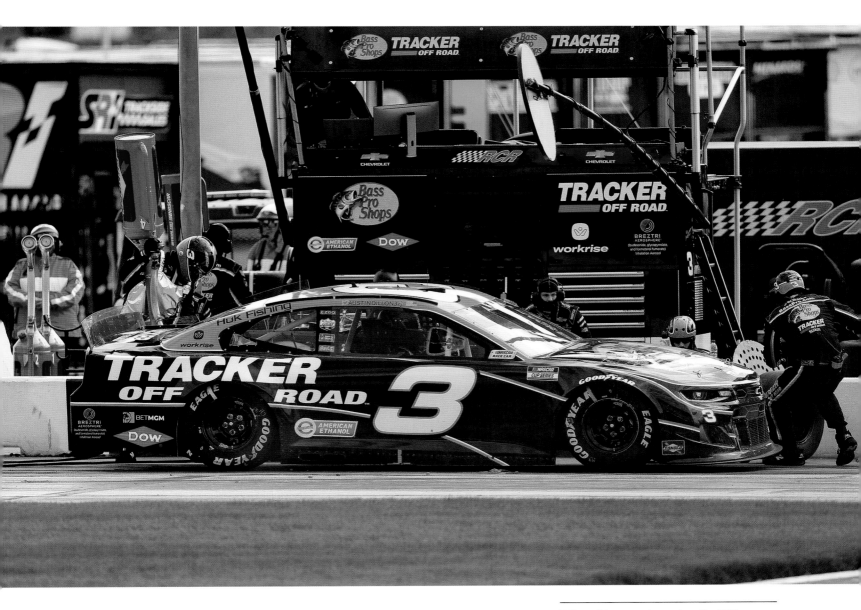

As for the green-and-white-checkered rule, NASCAR officials tweaked it after the Budweiser Shootout at Daytona ended under caution. Wanting fans to have a chance at seeing the ending of races under green flag conditions, the new policy gave three attempts at a green-and-white-checkered finish.

The Daytona 500 took over 6 hours to run. A pothole between Turns 1 and 2 caused a lengthy delay, and then Jamie McMurray emerged as the unlikely victor for Earnhardt Ganassi Racing. McMurray was a true feelgood story, and his Daytona win gave way to a Brickyard 400 win later in the year.

Kyle Busch became the answer to a future trivia question as the first driver to win three NASCAR races in a single weekend at the same location when he swept the Camping World Truck, Nationwide Series, and Sprint Cup Series races at Bristol Motor Speedway.

When his grandson Austin Dillon was ready to move to the Cup Series full-time in 2014, Richard Childress decided to bring back the iconic No. 3 for him to drive. Childress had not used the number since his good friend and Hall of Fame driver Dale Earnhardt was killed in a last-lap crash in the 2001 Daytona 500.

MUCH NEEDED MOVE

As technology in the real world changes rapidly, it often puts NASCAR in a position of playing catch up. While driving a race car to work isn't realistic, making the race car that fans enjoy watching on Sunday afternoons look like its passenger production vehicle counterpart is. And that means those cars need to have the same parts and pieces.

Going into the 2012 season, one of those areas long overdue for an update was around engine technology. NASCAR officials moved away from carburetors to fuel injection.

Carburetors had been used since NASCAR's inception in 1949. It was a device that sent a mixture of air and fuel into the engine of a Cup Series race car.

Electronic fuel injection—or EFI—is precisely how it sounds. Eight electronically controlled fuel injectors reside on the intake manifold and an onboard computer (ECU or Engine Control Unit) uses sensor input to calculate how much fuel needs to be added to the airflow going to an engine cylinder. It's a more precise and efficient fuel delivery system, and engine builders get more performance out of their engines because they have more data.

It was a technology that passenger cars had used since the 1980s.

Freescale Semiconductor and McLaren Electronic Systems became the suppliers of the fuel injectors for NASCAR teams.

"They'll sound the same, they'll run the same," said NASCAR vice president of competition Robin Pemberton. "They'll make the same horsepower, if not more. We'll have the same great racing we've had."

The only difference was in what the fans saw. No more would there be flames shooting from the side of the race car because there was no more raw fuel getting to the exhaust system.

The decision to move to EFI came after years of hesitation from the sport to move to an electronic system for fear teams would tamper or cheat the process. However, McLaren had experience supplying fuel injectors to race teams such as in open-wheel competition (IndyCar and Formula 1) and, as such, knew how to make tamper-proof products.

The move to EFI came on the heels of NASCAR making Sunoco its official fuel partner and having race teams use a 15% ethanol blend (E15) in 2011.

However, despite the move to EFI, NASCAR officials chose to keep restrictor plates on the cars. Restrictor plates were bolted underneath the carburetor to help slow the cars down on the superspeedway tracks of Daytona and Talladega. With EFI, the restrictor plates stayed and were bolted elsewhere to help control speeds.

With the switch from carburetion to electronic fuel injection for the 2012 season, the vehicle's engines looked a bit different, but the outward appearance of the cars themselves remained unchanged.

TANDEMS AND TIEBREAKERS

The 2011 season was bookended with two incredible stories.

NASCAR's oldest team went to victory lane in the Daytona 500 with a rookie. Trevor Bayne shot to stardom when he drove the No. 21 Wood Brothers Racing Ford to the win in Daytona. Bayne had a fast car all week and caught the attention of four-time champion Gordon, who didn't hesitate to draft the young driver.

Drafting help was more important than ever during this time. Drivers found that two cars could break away, leading to pack racing disappearing for pods of two.

It was Bayne's second career start. It was the ninety-eighth victory for the Wood Brothers in the Cup Series.

The season ended with the closest points battle in history as Tony Stewart became a three-time champion in a tiebreaker over Edwards. Stewart didn't win a race until the postseason began, and his five wins in ten weeks gave him the edge over Edwards' one.

After an on-track dustup at Kansas Speedway late in the 2015 season, the usually mild-mannered Matt Kenseth waited until a crucial moment two races later to exact revenge on Joey Logano. As Logano was trying for his fourth consecutive victory and leading on Lap 453 of 500 at Martinsville Speedway, Kenseth plowed into him and took him out of both the lead and the race. The incident slowed Logano's momentum in the championship chase, which Kyle Busch eventually won.

ABOVE LEFT: **As if being the son of Hall of Famer Bill Elliott wasn't pressure enough, Chase Elliott was also asked to be the driver who succeeded four-time Cup Series champ Jeff Gordon in the No. 24 car for Hendrick Motorsports. Over the course of two seasons in the No. 24, Elliott recorded twenty-two top-five wins and thirty-eight top-ten wins, but prior to the 2017 season, he switched to the No. 9 in honor of his father.**

ABOVE RIGHT: **Dale Earnhardt Jr. went to Victory Lane three times in 2015, and those were the last three wins of his Cup Series. After health issues limited him to just eighteen races in 2016, Dale Jr. returned to run the full thirty-six–race schedule in 2017, then retired at season's end and moved into the broadcast booth with NBC Sports.**

It is hard to argue with the idea that 2011 was one of the most exciting years in NASCAR history.

Bayne was the first of five different winners, including Regan Smith at Darlington for Furniture Row Racing, David Ragan at Daytona for Roush Fenway Racing, Paul Menard at Indianapolis for Richard Childress Racing, and Marcos Ambrose at Watkins Glen for Richard Petty Motorsports.

In all, there were eighteen different winners—the most since 2002.

HERE COMES KESELOWSKI

Keselowski pulled NASCAR into the social media era. Keselowski sent a shockwave through the industry by posting to Twitter from inside his race car during a red flag in the 2012 Daytona 500. Keselowski, parked on the backstretch, shared his view of the fire caused by the explosion of a jet dryer.

Yes, a jet dryer exploded in an unfortunate and unlikely series of events. The race was under caution, and Juan Pablo Montoya tried to catch the field. But something broke on his Chevrolet, sending him crashing in the same spot where a jet dryer was cleaning the track. The collision quickly turned into a giant fireball from the fuel spilled onto the racetrack. Both Montoya and the jet-dryer driver, Duane Barnes, miraculously were uninjured.

A week later, the incident had become a T-shirt, with crew members wearing shirts that read, "I love the smell of jet fuel in the morning."

NASCAR rolled out a new drying system a year later. The Air Titan trucks reduced track-drying time dramatically with a system that essentially vacuumed water from the racing surface.

As for Keselowski's tweet, it was heard around the garage. Not only did his follower count swell, but the engagement was also the beginning of NASCAR, its teams, and drivers realizing the need to embrace a new platform.

At twenty-eight years old, Keselowski went on to win the championship, his first and the first for team owner Roger Penske. The celebration was one for the ages. NASCAR's newest champion, who had just three career wins on his résumé, enjoyed the spoils of victory live on national television with a giant beer glass that made sponsor Miller Lite proud.

It was also a celebration for Dodge, which left the sport on top after a twelve-year run and fifty-five wins.

And yes, Keselowski tweeted a picture from inside his car after arriving at the championship stage.

Carl Edwards's signature move after each of his Cup Series wins was to climb onto his car and backflip off of it onto the ground. Race fans got to see the stunt twenty-eight times in his thirteen seasons before Edwards shocked the NASCAR world by retiring unexpectedly following the 2016 season, walking away from the sport entirely without explanation.

SAFER Barrier safety technology continued to evolve and improve throughout the decade and, most importantly, it continued to save lives and helped to protect drivers from serious injury. Here Joey Logano hits the wall hard after tangling with Elliott Sadler on the final lap of the NASCAR Xfinity Series race at Talladega Superspeedway on April 30, 2016. Fortunately the Safer Barrier allowed Logano to walk away from the spectacular crash.

After the 2016 Indianapolis 500, Tony Stewart and Jeff Gordon shared one final moment together on the track. Stewart would retire at the end of the season, and Gordon was subbing for an injured Dale Earnhardt Jr. in the No. 88 Axalta Hendrick Motorsports car. Before the race, Gordon had saluted his fellow Indiana native in the drivers meeting, calling on all those in attendance to "recognize what you have done for the sport." Stewart finished eleventh and Gordon thirteenth in their final Indy 500.

HERE COMES DRAMA

Tweaking the NASCAR playoff system became commonplace in the years following its inception.

It started as a simple 10-driver format that expanded to twelve drivers a few years later. A third tweak didn't change the number of drivers, it stayed at twelve, but the rules were different in that the final two spots went to the highest drivers in points who weren't already locked in.

The fourth version of the system, implemented in 2014, was the most dramatic, which was precisely the intention. Simply put, the postseason was now broken into three-race rounds with eliminations along the way.

To get there, a driver needed to win the first twenty-six races—the regular season—to earn a playoff spot. Instead of twelve drivers, it was now sixteen drivers.

The playoffs were the final ten races of the season but broken up into four rounds. Three races through the first three rounds with drivers advancing if they won one of those races. The lowest four drivers in points after each round was eliminated.

It left four drivers standing for a winner-take-all season finale. The highest finishing driver of the four championship contenders took the trophy.

Drama. Game 7 moments. That is what NASCAR was chasing with a format much like other sports.

"It's another PR deal, OK?" Petty said. "NASCAR wanted to do something to cause a little more interest in the way the point standings are viewed. I think I won championships with five different ways of counting the points. In the long run, no matter how you cut the points out, you're pretty well going to have the best guy winning the championship.

"It's just something different, just another change. Whether it's the right format or not, it's the format that football and baseball use and it's pretty successful there. So let's give it a try here."

From the start, NASCAR got what it wanted. Ryan Newman advanced into the championship finale race after bumping Kyle Larson out of the way on the final lap of the penultimate race for the position he needed.

Jeff Gordon earned the final win of his NASCAR career in 2015, advancing him into the finale with a shot at a fifth series championship.

The trend soon became that the eventual champion needed to win the final race to win the championship. Kevin Harvick started it off in the first year.

Suddenly the fall Martinsville race, the final cut race before the Championship 4 drivers are determined, became appointment television. The last chance to punch a ticket to the championship fight, drivers became more aggressive than ever to win the race or claim the finishing position they needed.

Joey Logano knocked Martin Truex Jr. out of the lead for the win in 2018 to earn his spot. A week later, Logano won the championship.

But while perhaps fun to watch, drivers became much more stressed trying to win a championship.

"I think it's harder," said Jimmie Johnson. "I think playoff-style is much more difficult, and I think there's been some good examples of it over the years where maybe a [title] favorite doesn't have what they need to in the final race or the final few races, and it swings the other way."

The 2014 reformatting of the playoff system made the fall Martinsville race the last chance for drivers to punch a ticket to the championship fight. In 2018 Joey Logano (22) knocked Martin Truex Jr. (78) out of the lead to earn his spot. A week later, Logano won the championship.

The first woman to run full-time in the Cup Series was Danica Patrick, a driver who was just as well known for her driving success as she was for being a highly visible spokesperson for her long-time sponsor, GoDaddy. com. Patrick ran 191 races over parts of seven seasons, and her greatest racing accomplishment was winning the pole for the 2013 Daytona 500. She also had seven top ten finishes to her credit, but never cracked the top five.

GIRL POWER

The 2013 season started with a boost from the Danica Patrick effect.

Patrick began her first full season in the Sprint Cup Series driving for Stewart-Haas Racing by winning the pole for the Daytona 500. She then became the first female to lead laps in the race on her way to finishing eighth.

Musical chairs for the drivers featured two significant changes. Matt Kenseth departed Roush Fenway Racing after fourteen seasons for Joe Gibbs Racing, while the driver he replaced, Joey Logano, got a second chance with Roger Penske.

Both would go to victory lane with their new teams. For Kenseth, it happened sooner than perhaps expected.

Kenseth won the third race of the year in Las Vegas and was back in victory lane a month later in Kansas. David Ragan scored an upset win for Front Row Motorsports at Talladega Superspeedway before Kenseth became a four-time winner with victories at Darlington Raceway and Kentucky Speedway.

Johnson swept the races at Daytona with a second win in the Daytona 500 and his first in the summer race. It was the first time since 1982 that a driver accomplished the feat.

A week later, Brian Vickers earned one for the underdogs with a win at New Hampshire for Michael Waltrip Racing. While it was the third career win for Vickers, it was the final win for MWR, as the worst was yet to come.

Logano was victorious at Michigan for Penske. In the end, it was his only win of the season but it was still the kick-start to a successful pairing, as Logano would begin picking up multiple wins in a season a year later.

A dark cloud hung over the sport going into the postseason. Michael Waltrip Racing driver Martin Truex Jr. was booted from a Chase spot when NASCAR penalized the organization for manipulating the outcome of the cutoff race at Richmond Raceway. Clint Bowyer intentionally spun to bring out a caution to help Truex's cause.

NASCAR's penalties were harsh enough (a fine of $300,000 and general manager Ty Norris indefinitely suspended). But sponsor NAPA was also pulling its support at the end of the season.

Ryan Newman took the spot Truex would have had, as he was the driver impacted by the ploy. Later in the week, Gordon was added as the thirteenth driver when NASCAR found Team Penske and Front Row Motorsports conspired to help each other, although to a lesser extent than the Waltrip team.

The championship chase began in Chicago but without the defending champion, Keselowski. Keselowski missed out on the postseason by going winless in the regular season. He'd win in the middle of the postseason at Charlotte Motor Speedway in what would only amount to a confidence booster.

Keselowski's absence was no matter to Kenseth, who drew first blood in the title hunt by winning at Chicagoland. Kenseth then threw another punch at the competition with a win a week later in New Hampshire.

Johnson got on the board by winning at Dover International Speedway and then Texas. In the finale two weeks later, Johnson, holding a twenty-eight-point lead on Kenseth, did all that was needed, with a ninth-place finish in the finale to take home his sixth championship.

"Unfortunately we're racing during the Jimmie Johnson era," said race winner Denny Hamlin. "We're just unlucky in that sense. Racing with him, I think he's the best that there ever was. He's racing against competition that is tougher than this sport's ever seen."

But if Johnson were ever going to win another championship, it would have to come under a completely different format.

Tony Stewart won forty-nine races and three Cup Series championships during his eighteen years as driver. He retired following the 2016 season to concentrate full-time on his duties as co-owner of Stewart Haas Racing, alongside other racing ventures, such as his ownership of the Eldora Speedway dirt racing facility in Rossburg, Ohio. In 2020 he teamed up with Ray Evernham to form the Superstar Racing Experience (SRX), winning its first championship as a driver in 2021.

Jimmie Johnson takes a victory lap after winning the Ford EcoBoost 400 at Homestead-Miami Speedway on November 20, 2016. It was the final race of the season, and Johnson's victory secured his seventh NASCAR championship. Given that Johnson also won five straight championships from 2006 to 2010, his 2016 championship win tied him with Richard Petty and Dale Earnhardt Sr. for the most championships in series history.

Denny Hamlin won twenty-nine races from 2010 to 2019, tying him with Brad Keselowski for the fourth highest total in the decade. Despite his victories, the closest he came to winning a Cup Series championship was when he earned a runner-up spot in 2010. Hamlin went to Victory Lane eight times that year but still trailed Jimmie Johnson, who wrapped up his fifth consecutive title by thirty-nine points at the season's end.

GO BIG OR GO HOME

If the first edition of the NASCAR postseason was a game-changer, the 2014 version ratcheted up the intensity. In late January, officials announced the final ten races would be broken up into three rounds with eliminations, a sixteen-driver field, and a finale with a winner-take-all scenario between four drivers, dubbed the Championship 4.

"We have arrived at a format that makes every race matter even more, diminishes points racing, puts a premium on winning races and concludes with a best-of-the-best, first-to-the-finish-line showdown race—all of which is exactly what fans want," said Brian France, then Chairman and CEO of NASCAR. "We have looked at a number of concepts for the last three years through fan research, models, and simulations and also maintained extensive dialogue with our drivers, teams, and partners. The new Chase for the NASCAR Sprint Cup will be thrilling, easy to understand, and help drive our sport's competition to a whole new level."

Pundits couldn't have asked for a better start to the season. In the return of the No. 3 with Austin Dillon and Richard Childress Racing, it was the son of the man who made the number famous, Dale Earnhardt Jr., for Hendrick Motorsports in victory lane at Daytona International Speedway.

Earnhardt's Daytona 500 win was the start of a shining year. Alongside crew chief Steve Letarte, the best of Earnhardt emerged with a Pocono Raceway sweep and an elusive victory at Martinsville Speedway.

Stewart-Haas Racing established itself as a new type of powerhouse with the additions of Kurt Busch and Kevin Harvick. Both drivers featured prominently in the season as Busch pulled off the Indianapolis 500 and Coca-Cola 600 double. While it ended with disappointment at Charlotte Motor Speedway due to a blown engine, the day started with all eyes on Busch's impressive sixth-place finish at Indianapolis.

Harvick, meanwhile, earned his first Cup Series title by winning the finale at Homestead-Miami Speedway. Having advanced into the Championship 4 with a win the week before at Phoenix Raceway, Harvick, nicknamed "the Closer," stormed to the lead and into the championship club with eight laps to go.

BUSCH BATTLES BACK

If there is a lasting image from 2015, it might be the mangled car of Joey Logano sitting in Turn 1 at Martinsville Speedway. Logano was the victim of an irate Kenseth, who had felt wronged by the Team Penske driver for weeks during the Chase for the Sprint Cup.

When Richard Petty was asked to be the honorary pace car driver for the 2017 Southern 500 at Darlington Raceway as part of NASCAR's official Throwback Weekend, he enjoyed it so much that he never wanted it to come to an end. Driving his iconic No. 43 Pontiac Belvedere, the very car he won the 1967 Southern 500 in, Petty paced the field for a few laps as requested, then went on a joy-ride for a few more laps on his own, deviating from the original plan. To get a smiling Petty off the track so the race could begin, NASCAR finally had to do the unthinkable and black flag "the King" at Darlington.

ONE-OF-A-KIND CREW CHIEF

Chad Knaus was called many things during his tenure as a Cup Series crew chief—Winner. Innovator. Champion.

Knaus was the mastermind behind the success of Jimmie Johnson and the No. 48 Hendrick Motorsports team. For 17 years, Knaus guided Johnson to wins (81 of them), including in the sport's most prestigious ones like the Daytona 500, Coca-Cola 600, Southern 500, and Indianapolis. He was there for all seven championships.

The Rockford, Illinois, native led with a ruthless work ethic and was unafraid to push the limits of the rule book. Critics would say Knaus was nothing more than a world-class cheater.

Knaus and Johnson were paired together in 2002 when Johnson was hand-picked by Jeff Gordon and Rick Hendrick. It was also the year Knaus made his way back to the company after some time away to serve as a crew chief at Dale Earnhardt Inc., Ray Evernham, and Melling Racing.

Knaus and Johnson were a dynamic duo no one was ready for. They won their fifth consecutive championship in 2010, a record that will likely never be broken. It was done two years after breaking the previous record of three consecutive, which Cale Yarborough had set.

Knaus is the only crew chief to win five straight championships. The sixth came in 2013 and the seventh in 2016. They succeeded no matter the rules, car, or championship format.

Seven championships put Knaus behind only Dale Inman, who won eight with Petty Enterprises.

The rise of Knaus is not that different from many others in racing. Introduced to the sport by his father, John, who raced in the Midwest, Knaus moved to North Carolina, where he did whatever it took to break into the sport. Once he did, Knaus spent the 1990s under the tutelage of Evernham.

Knaus and Johnson didn't go the distance together, however. Their partnership ended after the 2018 season, and Knaus spent his final years atop the pit box breaking in another young Hendrick talent. It was Knaus who took William Byron to the winner's circle for the first time in the 2020 summer race at Daytona International Speedway.

After 20 years in the garage, Knaus moved into a managerial role with Hendrick Motorsports. When the day comes, he will be a first-ballot NASCAR Hall of Famer and one of the most well-known and accomplished crew chiefs to have competed in the sport.

Chad Knaus (left) confers with driver Jimmie Johnson during practice for the Kobalt 400 at Las Vegas Speedway on March 4, 2016.

Brian France certainly enjoyed the rivalry; he threw fuel on the fire after the Kansas Speedway race in which Logano spun Kenseth for the race lead by telling SiriusXM NASCAR Radio it was an example of "quintessential NASCAR"—two drivers racing hard and doing what they needed to do late in a race.

But it was a missed opportunity of a season for Logano. He won six races, including the Daytona 500, and was on a three-race winning streak when his tangle with Kenseth occurred. It's possible Logano, who was leading the race, might have won four straight races and advanced into the championship round.

Or maybe the lasting image is defiant and determined Kyle Busch hoisting his first Cup Series championship trophy. Busch completed a comeback story for the ages after missing eleven weeks with a compound break of his right leg and a fracture of his left foot from a wreck in the season-opening Xfinity Series race. His unlikely comeback led to five wins.

Busch's climb to the top of the mountain was M&M's sweet. But not as sweet as it was for his manufacturer. For the first time and after many ups and downs, Toyota was a Cup Series championship team.

The Busch brothers seemingly shared headlines. Unfortunately for older brother Kurt, it sidelined him for the season's first three weeks. Busch was suspended before the Daytona 500 because of domestic-abuse allegations. He did not face criminal charges.

Busch was back to his winning ways with a dominating performance at Richmond Raceway by April. A win in Michigan gave Busch a pair on the season.

Winning came to an end for Earnhardt Jr. The superspeedway ace picked up victories at Talladega Superspeedway in the spring and the summer Daytona International Speedway race before earning his final Cup Series victory in the rain-shortened Phoenix Raceway event.

Running for owner Barney Visser and a Furniture Row Racing team based in Denver, Colorado, Martin Truex Jr. won eight races to capture the 2017 Cup Series championship. The victory was a gift from Truex Jr. to Visser, who would disband the team after the 2017 season due to the rising cost of competing in NASCAR. It was also special to Sherry Pollex, long-time girlfriend of Truex Jr. who battled ovarian cancer as the season progressed.

Gordon's final Cup Series win was magical. Gordon took advantage of the spat between Logano and Kenseth to win in the twilight at Martinsville, going manic in his celebration. Gordon hollered and fist-pumped as he stood alone on the frontstretch before an equally enthusiastic team joined in.

BIG BUSINESS

No bigger break in NASCAR tradition has happened than in January 2016 with the announcement of a charter system. Thirty-six teams were given guaranteed starting spots in every race and team owners more stability when the time came to sell their assets.

Coming into the year, NASCAR knew two things: Sprint was ending its entitlement sponsorship, leaving the sport without a major sponsor, and three-time champion Stewart was retiring. However, Stewart still had some magic left in him and so, too, did the racing.

Hamlin kicked things off by claiming his first Daytona 500 win and the first for Toyota in dramatic fashion with a last-lap pass. It came with a margin of victory of 0.01 seconds over teammate Truex.

Johnson picked up two wins in the first five races while reigning series champion Kyle Busch won at Martinsville Speedway and Texas Motor Speedway in back-to-back weeks. A few weeks later, Busch missed out on another victory when teammate Edwards pulled off the bump-and-run at Richmond Raceway.

At Charlotte Motor Speedway in May, Truex turned in one of the most impressive performances ever seen in the Coca-Cola 600. Domination was an understatement as Truex and Furniture Row Racing set a race record of 392 of 400 laps led (588 miles).

Later that month, Stewart knocked down one last Cup Series win. In a battle with Hamlin over the final few laps at Sonoma Raceway, Stewart used his aggressive side to push past Hamlin in the final corners.

Stewart also had an unexpected photo-op at Indianapolis. In his final race at his home track, Stewart enjoyed extra time on track after the race alongside Gordon. Gordon had returned to fill in for the concussed Earnhardt Jr., and the two Brickyard 400 winners rode side-by-side around the track on a cool-down lap, soaking up their race moments as drivers at the famed Speedway.

When determining the series champion, it wasn't Stewart or Hamlin front and center. Edwards led the most laps of the four contenders in the finale at Homestead-Miami Speedway but wrecked with fellow contender Logano with ten laps to go.

"That was the race of my life up to that point," Edwards said. "I just pushed the issue as far as I could because I figured that was the race. I could feel him (Logano) a little, and I just thought I'd clear him or force him to lift. I just thought I'd have a little more time. And that's how it ended."

Johnson capitalized on the opportunity—he and the No. 48 team didn't have the best car but stormed to victory and Johnson's record-tying seventh championship.

However, the biggest surprise from the season didn't come until two months later. Edwards shockingly announced his retirement in early January and virtually disappeared from the racing scene.

A TITLE FOR TRUEX

There are many different "eras" in NASCAR, but the 2017 season started a completely new one in terms of marketing when Monster Energy became the entitlement sponsor of the Cup Series. Just the third entitlement sponsor in its history.

Black and green, Monster's colors, took over the circuit, and Monster girls became prominent in victory lane. And there was no better start to the new partnership than Monster Energy going to victory lane in the Daytona 500, as it was still a primary partner of Stewart-Haas Racing and race winner Kurt Busch.

Busch and crew chief Tony Gibson were a picture-perfect reminder of what it means to win the biggest race of the year. The triumph was the first for both and they celebrated as such. Busch was nearly speechless afterward, and Gibson was caught on camera going mad atop the pit box.

Daytona was also the debut of NASCAR's latest idea to shake up the racing—through stages. NASCAR changed its points system by breaking up the race into three stages and awarding drivers who finish in the top ten in Stage 1 and Stage 2 extra points. Drivers who won a stage were awarded a playoff point toward the championship.

Logano failed to make the playoffs when his Richmond Raceway win was ruled "encumbered," after his car failed inspection because of illegal suspension parts. While Logano still got credit for the win, it didn't count toward postseason eligibility, and Logano was unable to earn his way into the playoffs on points.

His presence probably wouldn't have mattered as Truex and Furniture Row Racing had everyone else covered. Having become a Toyota driver in 2016, Truex continued to show his promise by tearing through the series at a record pace. Truex showed everyone how stage racing was done by winning four races in the regular season and taking eighteen stages.

The performance gave Truex claim to the newly created regular-season championship. As the best driver in the first twenty-six races, the performance gave Truex an additional fifteen playoff points, and he went into the postseason with a nearly insurmountable fifty-three.

Truex remained untouchable in the final ten weeks. He won the first playoff race at Chicagoland Speedway and then two of the three races in the second round (Charlotte and Kansas). He capped off his season by winning the season finale and the championship at Homestead-Miami for a total of eight wins and 2,253 laps led.

As Truex celebrated his first title, Earnhardt and Kenseth said goodbye to the series. Earnhardt felt ready to go out on his own terms, giving the No. 88 car to Alex Bowman while Kenseth was being replaced in the No. 20 at Joe Gibbs Racing by Erik Jones.

LOGANO STANDS TALL

Logano flipped the script a year after being left out of the championship hunt. While the 2018 season appeared headed to a showdown between the "Big 3" of Harvick, Kyle Busch, and Truex, Logano stood tall in the end.

Harvick, Busch, and Truex combined for twenty wins, including ten of the season's first fifteen events. It was no surprise when the winning ways continued, and those three were three of the Championship 4 drivers. Busch was also crowned regular-season champion.

Logano qualified for a title spot after roughing up Truex in the final cutoff race at Martinsville Speedway, using an aggressive bump and run to take the lead and the win. Logano was booed afterward, and Truex played into the crowd hype by saying Logano wouldn't win the war.

But Logano did. A week later, in the Homestead-Miami finale, Logano took down all three drivers for his first title.

Truex didn't get the ending he wanted for Furniture Row Racing, which closed its doors a year after winning the title. The cost of racing and being an alliance partner to Joe Gibbs Racing became too much for team owner Barney Visser.

Kasey Kahne ended his full-time career in 2018. He had battled health issues through the summer months and had to vacate his Leavine Family Racing machine at Indianapolis (and for the rest of the season) because of severe dehydration issues occurring during the long Cup Series races.

And then came the end for Brian France. Less than 24 hours after NASCAR finally saw Chase Elliott win his first race at Watkins Glen in a thrilling battle with Truex, news broke that France had been arrested in Sag Harbor, New York, on charges of aggravated driving while intoxicated and criminal possession of a controlled substance.

France stepped aside as Chairman and CEO and later pleaded guilty to DUI. His uncle, Jim France, took the helm of the family business, and the sport quietly moved onward.

Kyle Busch's second Cup Series title in 2019 looked nothing like his first, but neither did the racing.

OPPOSITE: **This may look like a pack of cars at Daytona International Speedway or Talladega Superspeedway, but it's a restart at Martinsville Speedway during the 2019 STP 500. NASCAR's oldest track is still very much alive and well, hosting Cup Series races twice a year. Starting in 2020, Martinsville's fall event became the critical cutoff race, whittling the championship playoff field from eight drivers to four for the championship final the following week.**

Martinsville Speedway was one of the eight tracks that hosted Cup Series events during NASCAR's inaugural season in 1949, and it remains on the schedule to this day, hosting Cup Series races twice a year. The .0526-mile facility was built in 1947, nearly a year before NASCAR was officially formed, making it one of the first paved oval tracks in all of stock-car racing. The track is also famous for the hot dogs it serves at its concession stands as well as the Norfolk Southern Railway tracks that are less than a football field's distance from the back straightaway.

NASCAR introduced two distinct aero packages with horsepower choked back for all racetracks over 1 mile at 550-horsepower and an 8-inch spoiler. The 750-horsepower package was used on short tracks and road courses.

Busch, not the biggest fan of the lower horsepower package, was nonetheless the class of the field. After winning two of the first five races, Busch won twice more in the regular season to claim a second straight regular-season championship.

Along the way, Bowman won his first race as a Hendrick Motorsports driver at Chicagoland. Justin Haley and Spire Motorsports did a rain dance in Daytona for an unlikely win, and Kurt Busch and Chip Ganassi went to victory lane together for the first time at Kentucky Speedway by getting the best of Busch's younger brother in a late-race duel.

Kyle Busch won the one that mattered, besting teammate Truex in the season finale to win the championship. Busch became the first repeat champion under the elimination playoff format, while the streak of the champion winning the final race moved to six consecutive years.

JIMMIE JOHNSON
(2010, 2013, 2016)

TONY STEWART
(2011)

CHAMPS

An improbable fifth consecutive championship for Johnson in 2010 gave him one for the thumb. Johnson won races by the bunch en route to doing so with back-to-back wins in California and Las Vegas, then later in the year at Sonoma and New Hampshire. In all Johnson won six races. Johnson was back on top in '13 for the sixth time. His season included a season-sweep at Daytona while becoming a two-time Daytona 500 champion and two wins in the ten-race Chase at Dover and Texas. Johnson wrote another page in the NASCAR history book with his record-tying seventh championship in '16. Of his five wins along the way, including in the Homestead-Miami championship race, Johnson also went to victory lane at Atlanta, California, Charlotte, and Martinsville.

Stewart and Carl Edwards delivered a barn burner of a title fight, which came down to the season's final race and a tiebreaker. A win by Stewart in the season finale tied him with Edwards in points but Stewart's five wins on the season gave him the championship over Edwards. All five of Stewart's victories came in the last ten races of the season.

(CONTINUED ON 202)

BRAD KESELOWSKI

(2012)

KEVIN HARVICK

(2014)

KYLE BUSCH

(2015, 2019)

The first new champion of the 2010s was underdog Keselowski. Despite driving for Roger Penske, Keselowski was unproven, with four career wins going into the season. But in '12, Keselowski won three times and traded the point lead back and forth with Johnson during the ten-week Chase. Keselowski finished fifteenth in the season finale to earn the championship, the first for the Penske organization.

Harvick was the last man standing in the first winner–take–all finale, doing so over title rival Ryan Newman. Harvick won five races in his first year with Stewart-Haas Racing, including three in the final ten weeks. It was a full-circle moment for the man who, ready or not, was brought into the Cup Series to fill the shoes of Dale Earnhardt.

Busch capped off his comeback season with his first championship. Busch missed the first eleven races of the season due to injury but won four races in five weeks before the postseason started. Busch triumphed on the Sonoma road course and then at Indianapolis for the first time. His fifth race win was in the championship-deciding race. Busch became the first repeat champion under the elimination–style format in '19. Busch was strong throughout the year, with four wins in the regular season at Phoenix, California, Bristol, and Pocono. The Bristol win was Busch's eighth at the track, making him the winningest driver. His fifth and final win came in the finale at Homestead–Miami to clinch the championship.

MARTIN TRUEX JR.
(2017)

JOEY LOGANO
(2018)

Truex dominated the series for his first championship. Truex won eight races on intermediate tracks like Las Vegas and Chicagoland to the Watkins Glen road course. He also led the way with twenty-sixth top-ten finishes and 2,253 laps led.

By winning the war over Truex, Logano became a first-time champion. Logano won three races, two of which at Martinsville and Homestead–Miami, came in the postseason. Logano bumped Truex out of the way at Martinsville to advance into the championship race and then beat Truex and Harvick to the checkered flag at Homestead for the title.

After nearly twenty-five years, the 1.54-mile Atlanta Speedway was repaved in time for the 2022 season and the resurfacing proved to be a huge success. William Byron won the first event on the beautiful new blacktop, taking the 2022 Folds of Honor QuikTrip 500 on March 20. The race featured forty-six lead changes and nail-biting side-by-side racing in large packs, much like the superspeed action seen at Daytona or Talladega.

THE 2020s AND BEYOND

Next (Gen)eration

By Kelly Crandall

ABOVE LEFT: **Ryan Newman was leading coming off Turn 4 on the final lap of the 2020 Daytona 500 when he was turned by Ryan Blaney and went airborne. The car flipped onto its roof and was then hit in the driver's side by Corey LaJoie. Newman was eventually taken to nearby Halifax Medical Center with serious, but not life-threatening, injuries. Two days later, he walked out of the hospital hand in hand with his two daughters.**

ABOVE RIGHT: **After twenty years and 686 races in the No. 48 Hendrick Motorsports Chevy, Jimmie Johnson ran his final Cup Series laps in 2020. Johnson finished his career tied with Richard Petty and Dale Earnhardt with seven Cup Series championships, including an unprecedented five consecutive championship victories. With a total of eighty-three wins, Johnson tied with Hall of Famer Cale Yarborough for most career victories.**

THERE WAS NO WAY of knowing that the start of the 2020s, with now only the NASCAR Cup Series existing after Monster Energy ended its entitlement sponsorship, would start with figurative and literal storm clouds.

The Daytona 500 went from sunshine and excitement and a visit from the sitting president of the United States to being halted after twenty laps because of unrelenting storms. By Monday night, Denny Hamlin had won his third Daytona 500, but did so with a muted celebration because fellow racer Ryan Newman's condition was unknown.

Involved in a violent last-lap crash in which his car went airborne and was hit by Corey LaJoie at full speed, Newman was immediately transported to a hospital. Miraculously the Roush Fenway Racing driver walked out of the hospital holding the hands of his daughters two days later.

Then came a turn of events that forever changed the world and the sport.

Covid-19 halted NASCAR racing for eight weeks. Haulers parked in the garage at Atlanta Motor Speedway were sent home as the coronavirus pandemic offered a stark reminder of a bigger picture than wins and losses.

When racing resumed, it seemed almost secondary to the numerous storms still to come.

There was no practice and qualifying. Suddenly the industry realized it could show up and race without preliminaries, and that's precisely what it did as one of the first professional sports back in action at Darlington Raceway, May 17.

Upon its resumption, the Cup Series saw a battle of wills between Kevin Harvick of Stewart-Haas Racing and Hamlin of Joe Gibbs Racing. The pair combined to win sixteen races.

At season's end, seven-time champion Jimmie Johnson retired for a new challenge in the NTT IndyCar Series. Clint Bowyer also hung up his helmet for a seat in the Fox Sports booth.

As the veterans moved aside, Chase Elliott took his seat on the throne as NASCAR's new champion. Already its most popular driver, Elliott became one of the youngest Cup Series champions at twenty-four years old.

ABOVE: **After what NASCAR deemed a racially motivated incident at the Talladega Superspeedway in June 2020, the entire garage lined up behind Bubba Wallace on pit road to show support for the Cup Series' only full-time African American driver.**

LEFT: **Great work on pit road helped Kevin Harvick, seen here in the red car in the first pit stall, win the Consumers Energy 400 and sweep a doubleheader weekend at Michigan International Speedway in August 2020. Harvick held off Brad Keselowski to win the Firekeepers Casino 400 on Saturday, then came back on Sunday to edge Denny Hamlin. That made Harvick the first Cup Series driver to win on consecutive days since Richard Petty in July 1971.**

Another young gun made headlines for all the wrong reasons. Kyle Larson was suspended just after Easter for using a racial slur while on the virtual racing simulator iRacing, which cost him his ride at Chip Ganassi Racing. Larson ran just four races before losing his job and being assigned to sensitivity training. Larson, however, went above and beyond to educate himself before applying for reinstatement and signing with Hendrick Motorsports.

NASCAR took steps forward in 2020 when forced into the spotlight on issues of racial equality and standing by one of its own. With the world changing, the NASCAR industry recognized the need to change its ways.

A RADICALLY NEW CAR

NASCAR's future is in the Next Gen race car.

It is a car built with the most up-to-date safety features and many modern pieces. Among those are single-lug nut wheels, independent rear suspension, rack and pinion steering, composition body, and a rearview camera. There is a noticeable shorter rear deck, lower roof, and wider dimensions.

And by giving each manufacturer more leeway in their designs, each car has a closer identity to its production counterpart.

Next Gen was necessary for the health of the sport. NASCAR and its owners admitted the business model was broken, and team owners needed a better way to cut costs long-term. Teams are now capped on their inventory (seven cars per team) instead of having the freedom to build a fleet of cars. And Next Gen is versatile enough to be raced on every type of racetrack.

Trackhouse Racing did just that and won. Ross Chastain won on the Circuit of the Americas road course in March 2022 and then used the same car to win at Talladega Superspeedway a month later.

"In my opinion, the importance of this car can't be over-stated," said NASCAR President Steve Phelps. "There are many things that Next Gen will do for us as a sport when it rolls out in 2022. The styling is going to be amazing. I think the racing is going to be better based on the aero-dynamics of the vehicle."

Trackhouse is one success story of Next Gen. Justin Marks founded the team after NASCAR announced its plans to introduce a new race car because Marks saw it as economically attractive.

February 2019 kicked things off when NASCAR announced plans for its new car. Later that year Austin Dillon became the first driver to test the car at Richmond Raceway in early October.

With the onset of the Covid-19 pandemic in the spring of 2020, NASCAR decided to push the car's rollout. Initially set for a 2021 debut, Next Gen instead stayed in development before hitting the track in 2022.

The car has been a significant variable for drivers and teams. Every piece under the skin of Next Gen is completely different, and it's taken time for teams to learn how to work on the cars while drivers are adjusting to a new challenge. Next Gen and its symmetrical body are hard to drive, leaving little room for error as drivers are spinning out more on their own.

But the car has produced tremendous racing at the intermediate tracks with the field closer together. It's also brought parity with different organizations frequently represented in the finishing results, and teams like Trackhouse have become major players in a short amount of time.

It is too early to tell and likely will need a year or more if Next Gen accomplishes the financial stability NASCAR and its teams are hoping for. But there is no denying it has delivered in its look and on-track product.

A good look at the Next Gen cars at the 2022 Daytona 500, featuring Chase Elliott (9) in the Chevy Camaro, Bubba Wallace (23) in the Toyota Camry, and eventual race winner Austin Cindric (2) in the Ford Mustang.

ABOVE: **For eighteen years, from 2002 to 2019, the Cup Series finale was run each season at Homestead-Miami Speedway. But during a schedule shake-up in 2020, the final race, which now serves as the championship race, was moved to Phoenix Raceway. It was there that Chase Elliott celebrated winning his first career Cup Series title on November 8, 2020.**

At Atlanta Motor Speedway in early June, the field sat idle on the front-stretch as NASCAR president Steve Phelps delivered an address on standing against racism. A few days later, before the green flag at Martinsville Speedway, where Darrell "Bubba" Wallace Jr. drove a Black Lives Matter car, NASCAR banned the Confederate flag from its properties.

Then came a noose found in Wallace's garage stall at Talladega Superspeedway. The FBI later determined it was not a hate crime. Still, the moment resulted in one of the most sobering and emotional images of the year, as other drivers and members of other teams marched behind Wallace's car as it was pushed to the front of the starting grid. The weekend events later drew a critical tweet from President Trump toward Wallace.

But NASCAR pushed onward with its most significant changes still to come.

THE STARS COME OUT FOR TEAM OWNERSHIP

Despite still operating under procedures put in place when the pandemic started, NASCAR entered the 2021 season embracing the excitement of change. And there was plenty of it.

New teams were ready to line up on the starting grid, and some featured owners of worldwide fame. NBA legend Michael Jordan launched a team—23XI

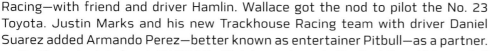

Racing—with friend and driver Hamlin. Wallace got the nod to pilot the No. 23 Toyota. Justin Marks and his new Trackhouse Racing team with driver Daniel Suarez added Armando Perez—better known as entertainer Pitbull—as a partner.

On the schedule front, NASCAR officials used words like "bold" and "dynamic," and for good reasons. New venues like Circuit of the Americas, Nashville, and Road America were added, and for the first time in over fifty years, the series competed on dirt with the revolutionary idea of throwing dirt over the racing surface at Bristol Motor Speedway.

The era of the sixth-generation race car came to an end in 2021. As the season started, teams knew a car that had been developed for two years, Next Gen was right around the corner.

When teams finally hit the track in Daytona, the prestige was still in the air, but there were many noticeable changes. For the first time in years, the grand-stands were not sold out—due to limited crowd capacity—and the same applied to a locked-down infield.

It didn't matter to Michael McDowell and Front Row Motorsports, as they became Daytona 500 champions. McDowell was in the right place at the right time when the Team Penske duo of Joey Logano, who was leading, and Brad Keselowski crashed going into Turn 3. McDowell, pushing Keselowski, avoided the fireball carnage for his first career win in the sport's biggest race.

A week later NASCAR celebrated another first-time winner. Christopher Bell looked like a veteran as he muscled his Toyota around the Daytona road course.

By early May and through the first eleven races, there were eleven different

PANDEMIC BRINGS CHANGE

The Covid-19 pandemic was a significant and historic event across the world and the sporting landscape. While NASCAR was no different, it had lingering effects on how the industry saw its weekend model, resulting in lasting changes.

NASCAR halted its season March 13 when haulers were already parked at Atlanta Motor Speedway. For eight weeks, there was no racing.

But NASCAR was one of the first professional sports to return to action in early May. It was of no surprise medical protocols were put into place, such as health screenings, masks, and limited infield access. Media members, only a handful, were restricted to the outside press box. Teams were limited in personnel at the racetrack.

The grandstands? Completely empty. NASCAR raced without fans on a case-by-case basis depending on the state the series visited that weekend. Some weekends the race was run behind closed doors, while other tracks welcomed limited spectators.

"I didn't think it was going to be that different, but it's dead silent out here," said Kevin Harvick after winning NASCAR's first race back. "We miss the fans."

One of the most significant differences was NASCAR adopting a show-up and race mentality that had never been seen before.

Officials made the unprecedented decision to do so without any practice or qualifying. Drivers would show up, walk to their cars, and charge into Turn 1 without any previous on-track time. What once seemed inconceivable became the new way of doing things.

NASCAR completed the 2020 season on time and got all of its races in. It wasn't without tweaks though. Doubleheaders were run, and races were slotted in during the week. Some tracks lost their race if the circuit could not travel to that state, but a full schedule of 36 events was put in the history books.

"(On Sunday), when we crown a champion in our Cup Series, we will have run all our races," NASCAR President Steve Phelps said. "We did it through ways that, frankly, probably we didn't think we could do, right? A bunch of midweek races. Three doubleheaders. No practice and qualifying. Things that were kind of significant in bedrock

that we do, right? You come to the racetrack, you're here for three days, you practice, you qualify, you're on your way, right?

"For us to be the first sport back without fans initially on May 17 in Darlington, to the first sport back with fans I think it's an extraordinary achievement."

In 2021 NASCAR carried much of the same format forward. Only significant races like the Daytona 500, Coca-Cola 600, the championship finale, and others had practice and qualifying. Eight events in all while the majority of the schedule again seeing teams show up and race without track time.

The less is more approach continues today. While practice and qualifying are back for all events, NASCAR has limited track time to a scant 20 minutes of practice before qualifying. It is the only time teams get to log laps before a race.

And three-day weekends? Those are mostly a thing of the past as well since most Cup Series events have been condensed to two days of track activity.

Driver John Hunter Nemechek walks pit road prior to the Real Heroes 400 at Darlington Raceway on May 17, 2020. NASCAR had just resumed the season after the nationwide Covid-19 lockdown.

winners. Some of the parity came from the freeze on parts and pieces, as teams were no longer able to develop new stuff because of Next Gen. While the big teams remained the powerhouses, the gap closed some to allow those like McDowell to put together a career year.

Except it also frustrated others because there was only so much that could be done. Ford went from dominating in 2020 to winning just seven races in 2021, but none came from Harvick. For the first time in twelve years, Harvick went winless.

Larson flexed his muscle early and often. Brought back into the Cup Series by Rick Hendrick and driving the No. 5, Larson and crew chief Cliff Daniels quickly established themselves as the best in class. Larson dominated week in and week out and won his first race with Hendrick in the season's fourth event.

On his way to winning the regular-season championship, Larson won the Coca-Cola 600, in his home state of California, at Sonoma, and the inaugural race at Nashville Superspeedway. His summer stretch was impressive, with three straight points-paying wins but four straight overall with the All-Star Race.

Larson's win in the 600 was also a milestone for team owner Rick Hendrick, as Hendrick Motorsports became the winningest team in the Cup Series. The victory was their 269th, which broke a tie with Petty Enterprises.

The only story bigger than Larson was the May 5 arrival of the Next Gen race car. After two years of hype, NASCAR and its three manufacturers rolled out their cars in a grand unveil in Charlotte, North Carolina. All three were striking for their close resemblance to their production vehicle counterpart.

In August, Marks provided some shock and awe of his own when he and Chip Ganassi walked into the great hall of the NASCAR Hall of Fame to announce Marks had bought out Ganassi. After three decades in stock car racing, Ganassi heard an offer he couldn't refuse and walked away after the November finale.

BELOW LEFT: **In an effort to add some variety to the Cup Series schedule, NASCAR and the promoters at Bristol Motor Speedway decided to turn the .533-mile facility into a dirt track for the spring 2021 race. More than 23,000 cubic yards of dirt were hauled to the track and put in place so the Cup Series could take place on dirt for the first time since 1970. Here Ryan Preece (37) kicks up a plume of dust as he tries to pass Cole Custer (41) and Chase Elliott (9).**

BELOW RIGHT: **With the introduction of its Next Gen car into the Cup Series in 2022, NASCAR made several radical changes to the vehicles seen on track. One of the most visible changes, and most hotly debated among many NASCAR fans, was the introduction of wheels that used single center-locking lug nuts. The aluminum wheel replaced the steel five-lug wheel NASCAR had used for decades.**

Daniel Suarez carries a Mexican flag to present to members of his fan group, Daniel's Amigos, who were there to see him become the first Hispanic driver to win a Cup Series race. Suarez took the lead with twenty-six laps to go in the Toyota/Save Mart 350 at Sonoma Raceway on June 12, 2022. He held on for the rest of the race and scored his first career victory. Suarez became just the fifth foreign-born driver to win a Cup Series race.

NASCAR has set its path forward with a radically different race car and arms open for what it could mean.

Teams like Trackhouse Racing and 23XI Racing have expanded, NASCAR continues to think of new and exciting ways to deliver its product, and Keselowski is now a co-owner and driver at the rebranded Roush Fenway Keselowski Racing.

The 2022 season-opening Daytona 500 was heralded for its energy. Fans and VIPs were back in force with sold-out grandstands, camping, and hospitality areas. Even better, the race went off without delay; rookie Austin Cindric held off veterans like Keselowski and Ryan Blaney.

Television numbers are strong, the schedule is changing, and the Next Gen car is an intriguing storyline. It is a car with modern features: independent rear suspension, sequential shifter, rearview mirror camera, forward number placement, symmetrical body, and a single center-locking lug nut. A new engine package is likely to come in the next few years, and NASCAR hopes new team owners and manufacturers will follow.

Joey Logano is becoming the king of firsts in NASCAR. In 2021, he was the inaugural winner of the Bristol dirt race, and in 2022 followed it by being the first winner at the Los Angeles Memorial Coliseum and at World Wide Technology Raceway in the Cup Series' first visit to St. Louis. It was only natural

ABOVE: **NASCAR's concerted effort to add more road races to its schedule continued during the early part of the decade. After turning Charlotte Motor Speedway's second race of the year into a road-course race in 2018, NASCAR ran on the road course in Daytona in 2020 and expanded its schedule to include seven road-course events in 2021 and five in 2022. Here a mad scramble of cars tries to navigate one of the hairpin turns on the 3.4-mile road course at the Circuit of the Americas in Austin, Texas, on March 27, 2022.**

RIGHT: **Ross Chastain emerged as a noteworthy driver early in the decade because of his hard-charging, take-no-prisoners driving style that led to notable on-track encounters with several veteran drivers. He is also well-known for a unique racing tradition inspired by his family's ownership of one of the largest watermelon farms in the world, located in Florida. As has been his custom throughout his racing career, Chastain prepares to smash a watermelon on the track after winning at the Talladega Superspeedway for the first time in his career on April 24, 2022.**

that Logano bookended 2022 with a victory at Phoenix Raceway to become the first repeat champion since Kyle Busch in 2015 and 2019.

"I knew going into this thing that we're going to win the championship," Logano said. "I told the guys we were the favorite from Daytona, and we truly believed it, and that's the difference."

RIGHT: **Erik Jones shocked everyone, including all sixteen playoff drivers, by going into the lead late and holding off hard-charging Denny Hamlin to win the 2022 Southern 500 at Darlington Raceway on September 4, 2022. Driving for Petty GMS Motorsports, Jones put the iconic No. 43 into Victory Lane at "the Lady in Black" for the first time since his boss Richard Petty won the Southern 500 in 1967—one of Petty's NASCAR record twenty-seven victories that season.**

BELOW: **Joey Logano crosses the finish line to win the 2022 NASCAR Cup Series Championship at Phoenix Raceway on November 6, 2022, bookending his earlier victory at the Los Angeles Memorial Coliseum.**

CONTINUED LEGACY

Jim France, the son of NASCAR founder Bill France Sr., took the reins of the family business following the departure of his nephew Brian in late 2018. Brian France, who served in the role from 2008.

Jim France was already visible to the industry even if the average fan couldn't pick him out of a lineup. France has been described as calm, down-to-earth, and always observing.

Under France's leadership, the sanctioning body has seriously listened to and worked on addressing the concerns of its stakeholders. Just months after France took charge, officials announced plans to build a new car—and went to work collaborating with the garage on Next Gen, the sport's radically new and said to be an important race car.

"The thing that I have learned about Jim—I didn't know Jim very well before he took charge—but the thing that I have learned about Jim is he's a race fan in a big way. Loves racing," said Kevin Harvick

Sports car racing is another passion of France. He founded GRAND-Am Road Racing and was a voice behind the merger of the GRAND-Am and American Le Mans series. In addition to overseeing NASCAR, France also oversees American Flat Track.

In June 2022, France was awarded the Spirit of Le Mans Award, recognizing those who uphold the values of enduring racing by their commitment, team spirit, and competitive drive.

It was a fitting tribute to France as he is a driving force behind NASCAR returning to Le Mans in 2023 to compete in the prestigious 24-hour race. The last time NASCAR was there was in 1976, when Bill France Sr. and the race organizers allowed two stock car entries for NASCAR drivers. Next year Jim France looks at the event as the perfect place to showcase the Next Gen car and introduce NASCAR to a new fan base.

Jim France, son of NASCAR founder Bill France Sr., took the reins of the family business in late 2018. Under his leadership, the sanctioning body has worked to address the concerns of its stakeholders.

ABOUT THE WRITERS

KELLY CRANDALL has been on the NASCAR beat full-time since 2013, and joined RACER.com as chief NASCAR writer in 2017. Her work has also appeared on NASCAR.com, NBC Sports, and in NASCAR Illustrated magazine. A corporate communications graduate from Central Penn College, Crandall is a two-time George Cunningham Writer of the Year recipient from the National Motorsports Press Association (NMPA) and currently serves as the organization's president. She is also a regular co-host on SiriusXM NASCAR Radio.

JIMMY CREED was born and raised in Talladega, Alabama, and started going to the track there at an early age. As the sports editor of The Anniston Star in nearby Anniston, Alabama, he twice received Alabama Sports Writer Association Story of the Year honors for stories written about the HANS Device and Davey Allison. He is the author of Donnie Allison: As I Recall, the official biography of the famed Alabama Gang member. A 1989 graduate of the University of Alabama in journalism, he also served as the editor of Saints Digest, the official publication of the New Orleans Saints from 1992 to 1996. He currently resides in Talladega.

MIKE HEMBREE has written about motorsports for four decades and is the author of fourteen books, including 100 Things NASCAR Fans Should Know & Do Before They Die. He has won numerous awards, including the American Motorsports Media Award of Excellence. He also is a seven-time National Motorsports Press Association Writer of the Year and a three-time winner of the Russ Catlin Award for motorsports journalism excellence. Hembree has covered auto racing for Autoweek, USA Today, the Greenville News, the Spartanburg Herald-Journal, the SPEED Channel, and NASCAR Scene. His news media career also includes coverage of the NFL, the NBA, MLB, the Olympics, and professional golf. Mike lives in Gaffney, South Carolina.

AL PEARCE saw his first NASCAR race in 1966 in Daytona Beach and covered his first race in July 1969 at Dover, Delaware for the Times-Herald of Newport News, Virginia. Since then, he's covered thousands of NASCAR, IndyCar, Formula One, NHRA, and SCCA races for the Tribune Company (1969-2004) and Autoweek (1973-current). Pearce has authored thirteen books on racing, including Unseen Earnhardt: The Man Behind the Mask and Holman-Moody: The Legendary Race Team (with Tom Cotter). He lives in Newport News, Virginia.

IMAGE CREDITS

INDEX

A

Advance Auto Parts 500, 170
Alabama, 40, 42, 55–58, 61–63, 69, 71, 75, 93, 98, 102
Alabama 500, 71
Alabama Gang of racers, 51
Allen, Johnny, 48
Allison, Bobby, 51, 58, 70, 75–76, 79, 82, 84, 86, 90–91, 94, 98, 103, 108, 111, 114, 116–118, 120–122, 139
Allison, Clifford, 139
Allison, Davey, 111, 114, 117–118, 127, 131–133, 139, 141, 149
Allison, Donnie, 55, 85–87, 90–91, 94, 133
All-Star Race, 91, 154, 171, 213
Ambrose, Marcos, 186
American 500, 77
American Le Mans series, 217
Andretti, Mario, 42, 49
Arford, Frank, 18
Arrington, Buddy, 96, 120
Asheville-Weaverville, 27
Atlanta, 40, 48, 54, 117, 129–130, 133, 135, 153–154, 162, 168, 182, 204, 206, 210, 212
Atlanta 500, 38, 107, 117
Atlanta Journal 500, 115
Aust, Jim, 168
Auto Club Speedway, 163

B

Baker, Buck, 14, 23, 32, 35, 37, 50–52, 65, 69, 130
Baker, Buddy, 84, 90, 98, 106, 115
Ballard, Walter, 91
Barnes, Duane, 186
Bayne, Trevor, 167, 180, 185–186
Beach Road Race, 11–12
Beadle, Raymond, 120
Bear, Roger, 71, 77

Beauchamp, Johnny, 19, 25, 33, 42
Bell, Christopher, 211
Berggren, Dick, 89
Bernstein, Kenny, 121
Bickford, John, 130, 145
Bill Davis Racing, 155
Blaney, Ryan, 196, 206, 214
Bodine, Geoff, 108, 112–113, 119, 132, 134
Bonnett, Neil, 90–91, 101, 139
Bouchard, Ron, 101, 106
Bowman, Alex, 196, 198, 200
Bowyer, Clint, 191, 206
Brasington, Harold, 23, 29–30
Brasington, Harold, III, 23
Brickhouse, Richard, 42, 55–56, 58, 63
Brickyard 400, 88, 132, 134, 149, 163, 172, 197
Bristol, 40, 46, 84, 99, 107, 117, 121, 123, 128–130, 147, 155, 157–158, 166, 178, 183, 202, 211, 213
Broderick, Bill, 141
Brodrick Bill, 73
Brooks, Dick, 76, 91
Broward Speedway, 17
Bud Moore Engineering, 35
Budweiser Shootout, 183
Burton, Jeff, 138, 141, 180
Burton, Ward, 138, 156, 166–167
Busch, Kurt, 195
Busch, Kyle, 157–158, 160, 163, 166–171, 173, 177–178, 182–183, 185, 193, 195–198, 200, 202
Busch Clash, 105–106
Busch Light Clash, 214
Busch Series, 130, 152
Busch Volunteer 500, 99
Byron, Robert "Red," 13–15, 20, 31, 37
Byron, William, 194, 196, 204

C

California Speedway, 173
Camping World Truck Series, 115, 178, 183
Car of Tomorrow (COT), 157, 164, 166–167, 180
Cardinal 500, 60
Carolina 500, 115
Carolina Dodge Dealers 400, 169
Champion Spark Plug 400, 118
Champion Speedway, 25
Charlotte, 10, 12, 14, 40, 51–53, 58, 60, 77, 90–91, 93, 112, 123, 131–132, 141–142, 154, 156, 160, 171, 191, 193, 196, 215
Chase for the Championship, 160, 177
Chastain, Ross, 171, 208, 215
Checker 500, 119
Chicagoland, 154, 182, 191, 198, 200
Childress, Richard, 99–100, 112, 114, 116, 148, 153, 162, 183
Chip Ganassi Racing, 156, 171, 207
Christian, Sara, 16
Cindric, Austin, 208–209, 211, 214
Clements, Louis, 65
Coca-Cola 600, 91, 103, 132, 142, 146, 193–194, 196, 212–213
Coke Zero 400, 136
Columbia Speedway, 28
Compton, Stacy, 156
Consumers Energy 400, 207
Cope, Derrike, 130
Covid-19 pandemic, 206, 212
Cracker Barrel Old Country Store 500, 162
Cracker Jack Track, 145
Craven, Ricky, 158–159, 169
Crawford Brothers, 76
CRC Chemicals 500, 101
Crider, Curtis, 46
Cronkite, Will, 84
Cup Series Coke Zero Sugar 400, 50
Custer, Cole, 213

D

Dale Earnhardt Inc., 154, 160–161, 194
Daniels, Cliff, 213
Darlington, 23, 29–30, 35, 37, 60, 83, 112, 119, 126, 137, 141, 149, 156, 158–159, 169, 176, 186, 190, 193, 206, 212, 216
Davis, Bill, 156
Daytona, 19, 25, 30–34, 40, 42, 46, 50, 66, 68, 78, 80–82, 100, 105, 107, 111, 113, 116–117, 127, 131–132, 136, 141, 144–146, 164, 182, 193–195, 211, 216
Daytona 500, 19, 32–34, 36, 42–44, 47, 49, 52, 60, 63, 66, 68, 71–72, 81, 85–86, 88–89, 91, 94, 98, 103–106, 112, 115–118, 127, 129–130, 132, 139–140, 142–143, 146, 148, 150, 154–156, 158–160, 163–164, 166–167, 171, 177, 180, 183, 185–186, 190, 193–197, 201, 206, 208–209, 211–212, 214
Daytona Beach & Road Course, 8, 15, 22, 24
DeCaires, Greg, 145
Dennis, Bill, 91
Dewar, Brent, 80
DeWitt, L. G., 84
DieHard 500, 133
DiGard Racing, 84, 100
Dillon, Austin, 183, 193, 208
Dixie 400 Cup, 48
Donohue, Mark, 91
Dorton, Randy, 160
Dover, 40, 82, 87, 101, 108, 126, 141, 155, 165, 176, 191, 201
Dunaway, Glenn, 12, 17
Dura Lube 400, 160–161

E

Earles, Clay, 55, 60
Earnhardt, Dale, Jr., 27, 122, 142, 146–147, 150, 154–156, 158–160, 163–164, 168–170, 173, 186, 188, 193, 195, 197–198

Earnhardt, Dale, Sr., 27, 84, 90–91, 96, 98–100, 112–117, 120, 122–124, 126, 128–132, 140, 142–144, 147–148, 150, 152–153, 158–159, 161–162, 164–165, 174, 183, 192, 206
Earnhardt, Ralph, 27, 120, 122
Earnhardt, Teresa, 164, 169, 171
Earnhardt Ganassi Racing, 183
Edwards, Carl, 157, 168, 170, 182, 185, 187, 196–197, 201
Elder, Ray, 91
Elder, "Suitcase" Jake, 92
Eldora Speedway, 191
electronic fuel injection (EFI), 184
Elliott, Bill, 84, 90, 102–104, 111–113, 115–116, 122–123, 137, 156, 186
Elliott, Chase, 186, 196, 198, 206, 208–210, 213
Elliott, Dan, 90
Elliott, Ernie, 90
Elliott, George, 84, 90
Evernham, Ray, 130, 148, 155–156, 160, 191, 194

F

Figaro, Lou, 18
Fireball 300, 59
Firecracker 400, 60, 78, 82, 94, 108, 110–111, 113–114
Firekeepers Casino 400, 207
Firestone Tire & Rubber Company, 56, 62, 77
First Union 400, 140
Flock, Bob, 15
Flock, Fonty, 14, 23
Flock, Tim, 17–18, 26, 31–32, 36
Folds of Honor QuikTrip 500, 204
Ford EcoBoost 400, 192
Foster, Billy, 53
Foster, Jim, 71

Fox, Ray, 52
Fox, Ray, Sr., 59
Foyt, A. J., 61, 66, 88
France, Bill, Jr., 30, 75, 80, 104, 147, 164
France, Bill, Sr., 11–19, 22, 31–32, 55–56, 58, 60–63, 69, 71, 75, 79–80, 141, 147, 164, 217
France, Brian, 80, 193, 195, 198, 217
France, Jim, 80, 198, 217
Freescale Semiconductor, 184
Front Row Motorsports, 191, 211
Fryar, Fred, 21
Furniture Row Racing, 186, 195–196, 198

G

Ganassi, Chip, 171, 200, 213
Gant, Harry, 90, 110, 123, 126, 141
Gatorade Duel, 145
Geico 400, 182
Gibbs, Joe, 141–142, 146, 149, 154, 176
Gibson, Tony, 197
Glotzbach, Charlie, 55
Goldsmith, Paul, 25, 28, 44
Goodyear Tire and Rubber Co., 53, 56, 62, 77
Goody's 500, 129
Goody's Headache Powder 500, 147
Gordon, Jeff, 124, 126, 129–130, 132–134, 137–138, 140–141, 144–145, 148–149, 155–156, 160–162, 164–166, 173, 176–177, 180, 182, 185–186, 188–189, 191, 194, 196–197
Governor's Cup, 88
Grand National, 70–72, 81–82
GRAND-Am Road Racing, 217
Grant, "Crash," 77
Gurney, Dan, 44, 61
Guthrie, Janet, 84

H

Haas, Gene, 173
Hagan, Billy, 149
Haley, Justin, 200
Hall of Fame, 181
Hall of Fame Cup Series, 170
Hamilton, Pete, 63, 71, 91
Hamlin, Denny, 191–192, 196–197,
    206–207, 211, 216
Harley J. Earl Trophy, 167
Harvick, Kevin, 154, 156, 162, 193, 198,
    202, 206–207, 212–213, 217
Heinz Southern 500, 126
Helton, Mike, 80, 142, 147
Hemi engine, 44
Hendrick, John, 160
Hendrick, Rick, 108, 119–120, 130, 160,
    168, 170, 194, 213
Hendrick, Ricky, 160
Hendrick Motorsports, 95, 108, 113, 119,
    140, 148–149, 160, 169–170, 173, 186,
    188, 193–194, 196, 200, 206–207, 213
Hickory, 18, 149
Highway A1A, 11, 13, 83
Hill, Bruce, 91
Holman-Moody, 42, 49, 59, 64, 68, 74, 84
Homestead-Miami, 139, 170, 177, 192,
    197–198, 201–203, 210
Hooters 500, 129–130, 133
Hudson, 31
Hyde, Harry, 94, 118–119, 121
Hyder, David, 166
Hylton, James, 64, 70–71, 84, 91

I

Indianapolis, 19, 22–23, 32, 132, 134,
    163–164, 168, 172, 176, 186, 197
Indianapolis 500, 23, 61, 171, 188, 193
Inman, Dale, 29, 43, 94, 114, 130, 138, 194
Interstate Batteries 500, 141
Irvan, Ernie, 139–141
Irwin, Kenny, Jr., 152
Isaac, Bobby, 64, 70, 84, 90–91, 94

J

Jackson, Joe, 160
Jackson, Keith, 115

Jacksonville 200, 50
Jarrett, Dale, 117, 132, 141–142, 159, 172,
    175
Jarrett, Ned, 38, 42, 44–45, 51–54,
    64–65, 81, 90, 115, 132, 141, 149
Jenkins, Bob, 115
Jiffy Lube 300, 141
Joe Gibbs Racing, 153, 167–168, 170,
    172–173, 190, 198, 206
Johnson, Jimmie, 95, 158, 160, 163–165,
    173–174, 177, 182, 189, 191–192, 194,
    196, 201, 206
Johnson, Joe Lee, 58
Johnson, Junior, 28, 33, 38, 42, 51–54,
    60, 71, 74, 92, 95, 100, 103, 120
Jones, Erik, 198, 216
Jones, Possum, 24
Jordan, Michael, 210–211
Joy, Mike, 115
Junior Johnson and Associates, 35, 84,
    91

K

Kahne, Kasey, 160, 198
Kansas, 156, 158, 185, 195
Kennedy, Bobby, 166
Kenseth, Matt, 154, 156, 158, 160, 177,
    185, 190, 195–196, 198
Kentucky, 190, 200
Keselowski, Brad, 157, 182, 186–187,
    191–192, 202, 207, 211, 214
Kiekhaefer, Carl, 26, 31–32
Kite, Harold, 53
Knaus, Chad, 163, 165, 174, 182, 194
Knaus, John, 194
Krauskopf, Nord, 70, 84, 94
Kulwicki, Alan, 117, 119, 123, 129–130, 137,
    139, 149

L

Labonte, Bobby, 153–154, 176
Labonte, Terry, 43, 96, 101, 106, 109, 123,
    128–129, 135, 139–140, 147, 149, 153,
    169, 176
LaJoie, Corey, 206
Lakewood, 14–15, 20
Langhorne, 18, 27
Larson, Kyle, 171, 189, 207, 211, 213

Las Vegas, 158, 177, 190, 194
Latford, Bob, 104
Lathum, Scott, 160
Le Mans, 45
Leavine Family Racing, 198
Leffler, Jason, 171
Letarte, Steve, 193
Littlejohn, Joe, 13–14, 22
Lockhart, Frank, 11
Logano, Joey, 163, 185, 188–190, 193,
    195–198, 203, 211, 214
Lorenzen, Fred, 38, 42, 44, 51, 53–54
Lowe's Motor Speedway, 146–147, 167
Lund, Dewayne Louis "Tiny," 42, 44, 49

M

MacDonald, Arthur, 10
MacDonald, Dave, 53
Macon 300, 43
Mahoney, Chuck, 23
Makar, Jimmy, 154
Mann, Larry, 18
Manning, Skip, 91
Mantz, Johnny, 23, 30, 83
Marchbanks, 40
Marcis, Dave, 84, 91
Marks, Justin, 171, 208, 211, 213
Marlin, Sterling, 90, 134, 155–156,
    166–167, 171
Marmor, Don, 107
Martin, Mark, 100, 117, 140, 158, 173, 176
Martinsville, 41, 52, 54–55, 60, 79, 82,
    108, 126, 129, 141, 160, 170, 180, 185,
    189, 193, 196, 198–200, 203, 210
Matthews, Banjo, 22, 74
Mayfield, Jeremy, 160
MBNA Cal Ripken Jr. 400, 165
McDowell, Michael, 157, 211, 213
McDuffie, J. D., 120, 139
McGriff, Herschel, 23, 74
McHugh, Clint, 18
McKim, Buzz, 74
McLaren Electric Systems, 184
McMurray, Jamie, 156, 167, 171, 183
McReynolds, Larry, 100, 102, 121, 127
McVitty, John, 18
Means, Jimmy, 102, 120
Melling Racing, 194

Memphis-Arkansas, 18
Menard, Paul, 186
Michael Waltrip Racing, 166, 175, 190–191
Michaels, Al, 115
Michigan, 31, 40, 82, 116, 118, 139, 155,
    170, 176, 190, 195, 207
Miller Genuine Draft 500, 132
Mineta, Norman Y., 157
Monster Energy, 197, 206
Montoya, Juan Pablo, 171, 186
Moody, Ralph, 74
Moore, Bud, 65, 105, 116
Morrison, Liz, 160
Motor Racing Network, 90, 111
Mountain Dew Southern 500, 137, 169
Myers, Bobby, 18

N

Nab, Herb, 60
NAPA 500, 154
Napier, 10
Nashville, 99, 213
Nashville 420, 99
National 500, 52
National Stock Car Racing Circuit, 14
Nationwide Series, 178, 183
Negre, Norman, 136
Nelson, Gary, 136
Nelson, Norm, 18
Nemechek, John, 139, 169, 212
New Hampshire, 141, 152, 155, 159, 177,
    190, 201
Newman, Ryan, 157–158, 160, 167, 189,
    191, 202, 206
Next Gen race car, 208–209, 211,
    213–215
Nextel Cup Series, 160
Nichels, Ray, 58, 63
Nixon, Richard, 68–69
Norris, Ty, 191
North Carolina, 40, 77, 130, 140, 160–161
North Wilkesboro, 28, 123–124, 141, 149

O

O'Donnell, Steve, 80, 164
Old Dominion 500, 52, 54
Ontario, 82–83
Orange Speedway, 41, 45

Sawyer, Billy, 77
Sawyer, Elton, 140
Sawyer, Paul, 77
Sawyer, Wayne, 77
Scott, Wendell, 22, 42, 45–46, 50–51
Seagraves, Ralph, 77
Seay, Lloyd, 20
Shelmerdine, Kirk, 148
Sicking, Dean, 153, 157, 168
Skeen, Buren, 53
Skinner, Mike, 139, 144
Smith, Bruton, 40
Smith, Jack, 14, 22–23, 31–32, 46, 58
Smith, Larry, 91
Smith, Louise, 16
Smith, Regan, 186
Sonoma, 196, 201, 213–214
Sony HD 500, 173
Sosebee, Gober, 8
South Boston, 83
Southern 500, 23, 29–30, 36, 60, 65, 74,
    91, 103, 112, 169, 176, 193–194, 216
Southern 500 Classic, 83
Sovran Bank 500 Cup, 108, 119
Spaulding, Paul, 28
Spire Motorsports, 200
Sprint Cup Irwin Tools Night Race, 178
Sprint Cup Series, 183, 190
Squier, Ken, 115
Stacy, J. D., 102, 114, 117
Stacy, Nelson, 44
Staley, Gwyn, 18
Stewart, Tony, 146, 158, 163, 167–168,
    172, 175–176, 185, 188, 191, 196–197, 201
Stewart-Haas Racing, 173, 190–191, 193,
    197, 202, 206
STP 500, 198
Streamline Hotel, 13–16, 79
Suarez, Daniel, 211, 214
Superstar Racing Experience (SRX), 191

T

Talladega, 40, 55–58, 62, 82, 93, 100,
    116–117, 132–133, 139, 152–153, 157,
    159–160, 168, 176, 181, 188, 190, 195,
    207, 210, 215
Talladega 500, 56, 62–63, 76, 84, 101,
    106, 114

Teague, Marshall, 13, 15–16, 31
Texas, 40, 82, 141, 154, 157, 180, 191, 196,
    201
Thomas, E. R., 10
Thomas, Herb, 14, 26, 32, 36
Thomas, Ronnie, 91
Thomas, Speedy, 21
Thompson, Speedy, 18, 26
Thompson, Tommy, 31
Toyota/Save Mart 350, 214
Trackhouse Racing, 208, 211, 214
Tracy, Dick, 160
Transouth 500, 119
Truck Series, 139, 152
Truex, Martin, Jr., 189–191, 195–198, 200,
    203
Turner, Curtis, 18, 23, 27, 31, 34–35, 40,
    61
Turner, Jeff, 160
Tuthill, Bill, 13–14
23XI Racing, 210–211, 214
Tyson Holly Farms 400, 124

U

UAW-GM Quality 500, 167
United States Auto Club racing, 130

V

Vandebosch, Ingrid, 145
Vanderbilt, William K., 10
Vandiver, Jim, 63, 78
Vickers, Brian, 190
Virginia 500, 54, 79
Visser, Barney, 195, 198
Vogt, Louis "Red," 13–14, 16
Volunteer 500, 46, 84

W

Wade, Billy, 53
Wallace, Bubba, 207–211
Wallace, Kenny, 152
Wallace, Rusty, 107, 117, 120, 123, 136,
    144, 158, 170
Waltrip, Darrell, 83–84, 88, 90–91, 98,
    100–104, 106–107, 109, 120–122, 136,
    154, 159–160, 163–164
Warren, Frank, 89
Warren, T. Taylor, 19

Watkins Glen, 120–121, 139, 186, 198
Weatherly, Joe, 18–19, 25, 42, 51, 53,
    64–65
Welborn, Bob, 19, 25, 27
Wells, Tommy, 46
Wheeler, H. A. "Humpy," 77, 90, 131
White, Rex, 18, 34, 45, 52, 65
Wickersham, Reb, 46
Wild World of Sports, 85
Wilson, Woodrow, 8
Winston 500, 71, 91, 98, 100, 102–103,
    111–112, 114, 116–117, 152–153
Winston Cup, 72, 75, 84, 114–115, 130,
    138, 141, 146–147, 153–155
Winston Million, 91, 103–104, 112, 152
Winston Racing Series, 82
Winston West 500, 71
Wolfe, Tom, 52
Wood, Glen, 25, 59, 61
Wood, Leonard, 59
Wood Brothers, 35, 49, 51, 59, 61, 78, 81,
    84, 101, 149, 155, 180, 185
Woods, Ernest, 20
World 600, 40, 53, 58–60
Wynette, Tammy, 109

X

Xfinity Series, 115, 182, 188, 195

Y

Yarborough, Cale, 42, 46–47, 51, 61, 74,
    77, 79, 82, 84–86, 88, 90–92, 94–95,
    103, 109–110, 170, 194, 206
Yarbrough, LeeRoy, 42, 51, 60, 71
Yates, Robert, 127
Yates Racing, 175
Yunick, Henry "Smokey," 20, 52, 74